# *Best Practices* for Planning Reading & Writing Instruction

**Antoinette Cerulli Fornshell**

---

New York • Toronto • London • Auckland • Sydney
Mexico City • New Delhi • Hong Kong • Buenos Aires

**Teaching** *Resources*

## Dedication

To Lynn Holcomb, who always pushes
me to ask one more question.

### Credits

Pages 14, 28, and 29: Reprinted by permission from *Guiding Readers and Writers, 3–6: Teaching Comprehension, Genre, and Content Literacy* by Irene Fountas and Gay Su Pinnell. Copyright © 2001 by Irene Fountas and Gay Su Pinnell. Published by Heinemann, a division of Reed Elsevier Inc., Portsmouth, NH.

Page 44: Reprinted by permission from *Creating Support for Effective Literacy Education* by C. Weaver, L. Gillmeister-Krause, and G. Vento-Zogby. Copyright © 1996. By Wynne Harlen. Published by Heinemann, a division of Reed Elsevier Inc., Portsmouth, NH.

Page 57: Tips included with permission of Fairfax County Public Schools, Fairfax County, Virginia.

Pages 68–80: "Units of Study in the Writing Workshop" by Isoke Titilayo Nia. Copyright © 1999 by the National Center on Education and the Economy.

Page 81: From *Strategies That Work: Teaching Comprehension to Enhance Understanding* by Stephanie Harvey and Anne Goudvis. Copyright © 2000. Reprinted with permission of Stenhouse Publishers.

Page 92: From *The Writing Workshop: Working Through the Hard Parts (And They're All Hard Parts)* by Katie Wood Ray. Copyright © 2001 by the National Council of Teachers of English. Reprinted with permission.

Cover design by Kathy Massaro
Interior design by Kelli Thompson
Photographs by Antoinette Cerulli Fornshell and Julie Droller
ISBN-13: 978-0-439-36596-3
ISBN-10: 0-439-36596-1
Copyright © 2006 by Antoinette Cerulli Fornshell.
All rights reserved. Published by Scholastic Inc.
Printed in the U.S.A.

1 2 3 4 5 6 7 8 9 10     40     14 13 12 11 10 09 08 07 06

# Contents

# Acknowledgments

I'd like to gratefully acknowledge that my work grows out of the work of so many.

Thank you to the wise teachers and administrators in Darien, Connecticut, who have opened their classrooms over these past two years and helped clarify the thinking that went into this book. Thank you especially to Julie Droller, language arts coordinator extraordinaire, who shared her thoughts, her time, and her photographs to help shape the vision of this book.

To Lucy Calkins, Isoke Nia, and the staff at the Teachers College Reading and Writing Project for continually stretching my thinking.

To the teachers at Roberts Avenue School, Danbury, Connecticut, and to the teachers in Connecticut's District 6. This book is filled with my learning from conversations with you, as well as with teachers at Stillmeadow School, Tracey School, Hayestown School, and Northeast School and the Fairfield Public Schools.

To the following teachers who graciously allowed me to photograph their classrooms:
- Shauna Riehl, third-grade teacher at Barlow Mountain School, who does such a great job teaching my son!
- Karen Dischinger, Lisa Whelan, Nancy Pires, and Rebecca Johnson at Barlow Mountain School.
- Karen Weber, Stacey Lange, and Julie Campbell, fourth-grade teachers at Springhurst School, Dobbs Ferry, New York.

To Jessica Cafiero, Jesse Diabola, and Nicole Mitura from Pace University for their help.

To Sarah Longhi, my editor at Scholastic, for guidance and support in editing this book. Because of you it's finished!

To Lynn Holcomb, for being a sounding board, first editor, supporter, and photographer—and mostly for being a great friend.

# Introduction
## Balancing the Need to Plan Ahead and to Continually Revise Our Ideas

*We need to get down to the essence of what we believe and what we do to ensure that our students become excellent readers and writers who choose to read and write. If we don't know how to teach reading and writing and move students forward, we must take responsibility for learning how. We must jumpstart our own professional development.*
*—Regie Routman,*
*Reading Essentials*

Over the years in my work as a staff developer, I have had the opportunity, the privilege really, to work alongside a countless number of teachers from a variety of different classrooms. I've worked in urban and suburban settings, with large school districts and small ones, schools where 60 percent of the population speaks a language other than English, and so on.

I've been able to see for myself how the latest research in literacy teaching is being translated in the real world. I've often thought how valuable those experiences and insights would have been if I were still teaching in the classroom full-time. Teaching can be such an isolating career. Some of us are fortunate enough to be working in a community that fosters collegiality and risk taking. Most of us are not, however. We close our doors and do what we do, alone.

The recent political fervor over "accountability" is scary. Society's ills are being blamed on schools. Policy makers are making rash decisions about school policies and practices based on knee-jerk reactions to public sentiment, which is being fed by the media. I've worked with teachers who have told me, "I want to include more independent reading and writing in my program, but you don't understand....My test scores were the lowest..." And, "They keep adding more to my curriculum; now I have to teach the character program. I just don't have the time to let the kids read and write." Where are our priorities?

I worked with a group of principals recently. We were taking a look at current best practices and considering how they, as educational leaders, could support the work in their schools. After listening to me describe what should be happening in intermediate literacy classrooms, one principal said, "I don't care how the teacher does it, just as long as she gets the job done." He didn't feel it was necessary to ask some teachers to change what they have been doing for the past twenty years, as long as they were getting high test scores. A comprehensive literacy program starts with a much broader definition of "getting the job done." Good test scores are important, especially in the politically charged arena that education has become. But how sad if that is our only measure of success in literacy teaching.

Literacy "giants" (Marie Clay, Donald Graves, Ken Goodman, Lucy Calkins, Katie Wood Ray, Sharon Taberski, Gay Su Pinnell, to name just a few) have spent years informing our literacy teaching. What I respect most about these educators is that they are constantly refining their work, based on what they see happening in classrooms. This can be overwhelming and even frustrating for those of us who don't like to feel like things are "always changing." But I've come to realize that this change is good. We need to stay up to date to avoid becoming stagnant and to provide the best instruction to our students. As long as we keep the ultimate goal of teaching the readers and writers in our rooms, as opposed to teaching a program or textbook, I think we'll continue to grow.

As a new teacher, so much of my energy was spent focusing on what I, the teacher, was doing. I read the teachers' manuals to tell me what to say and how to say it. I decided on what to teach based on the curriculum guidelines. Over time, though, I began attending summer institutes at the Reading and Writing Project at Teachers College. I began to read professional books on literacy learning. And my teaching changed.

I began to focus on the children, the learners. I learned to use running records, which informed my teaching. I paid attention to the students' needs and interests, which also informed my teaching. The bulletin boards in the room became more interactive. The students organized the class library. I added a writing workshop and a reading workshop.

Despite all the changes, I had a nagging feeling that I wasn't "getting to it all." So there is more balance to what I do now. I still focus on the children, but within a framework of an understanding of good literacy teaching. That's why I wrote this book, to help you walk the fine line between carefully framing curriculum while being open to new tides of ideas and the tug from students who require something different from what you planned.

This book grew out of my professional life, which now focuses on helping teachers make changes in their programs to develop readers and writers who read and write well—and because of that, do well on standardized tests. Although the work feels different in every school, with every group of children and with every teacher, there are basic truths, a vision if you will, that remains the same. This book is for teachers and districts who believe that

- all students can learn to read and write.
- students need to be taught strategies for reading and writing, not just given reading and writing assignments.
- there is a developmental continuum for learning to read and write, and teachers need to be able to assess students to determine where they fall on that continuum.
- authentic assessment should drive instruction.
- the best teachers are researchers of teaching and learning and continually outgrow many of their own ideas.

The most effective teachers are the ones who understand the difference between teaching readers and writers and assigning reading and writing. They have moved beyond merely covering the curriculum to focusing on the students. Districts spend a lot of time and money trying to find the "perfect program." There is no such thing. There are, however, accepted current best practices that are supported by research.

# What This Book Contains

In Part I , you'll learn why planning is so important in a comprehensive, balanced literacy program. It is not my intention to tell you what to teach and how to teach it, but rather how to use the process of planning to make the most of your methods. The idea of intentional teaching and how it best meets the true needs of our students while helping us feel in control will be the focus of Chapter 1.

Each of us has a different knowledge base and comfort level with teaching reading and writing. It is helpful to have a common language so we can have a dialogue. We're all learning more about literacy teaching all the time as we try to bridge the gap between what is and what should be. So in Chapter 2, I take a brief look at current best practices in comprehensive, balanced literacy programs.

Chapter 3, "Beginning Your Curriculum Binders: Using Units of Study to Plan Your Reading and Writing Workshops," provides an overview and examples of typical units of study in literacy for grades 3–5 classrooms.

If Part I of this book is about why to plan for the year in a comprehensive literacy program, Part II is about how. You will find step-by-step guidelines for planning your curriculum. Chapters 4, 5, and 6 describe how to begin with a yearlong plan and translate that plan into monthly and eventually daily lessons. I offer some ideas for professional development, accompanying reproducible forms, and a bibliography at the end.

Throughout this book, I'll ask you to carry out short writing tasks to help you think about and assimilate new information. If you are using this book as part of a professional discussion group, your responses will help guide productive conversations. Take the time to respond thoughtfully while working through the process of planning.

Katie Wood Ray, in her book *Writing Workshop: Working Through the Hard Parts (And They're All Hard Parts)*, reminds us not to lose sight of why we need to plan and to be articulate about our planning. Planning intentionally not only helps us explain ourselves better to others, but also informs our day-to-day teaching decisions because we'll be clear about what we are doing and why we are doing it. Katie's work and others' (including the work of Isoke Nia, former director of research and development at the Teachers College Reading and Writing Project) can give us the courage to stop asking for lists of 180 mini-lessons or a curriculum guide for workshop teaching and to start thinking for ourselves—to start asking, "What makes sense for me and the students in my classroom?"

Curriculum comes from a variety of places. Each state and district has its own mandates. There are new standards for literacy teaching all the time. Individual teachers have different expertise and interests. And then, of course, one has to consider the particular needs of the students in our classrooms. Over the years, I have been guiding teachers in creating curriculum plans for reading and writing workshops that balance all of these factors. My goal in writing this book is to help you be more intentional in your teaching and more purposeful in your planning as you work on putting it all together.

Part I
# Why Plan?

# Chapter 1

# The Power of Intentional Teaching
## How Does Your Current Practice Measure Up?

*We teachers have to be readers if we are to teach reading and writing well. Keeping a reading record is a great way to begin to keep track of our own reading. When teachers begin to keep their own reading records, they stop worrying about book levels and the number of pages and number of minutes students read each day. That carries over to students, who also stop focusing on how many pages they've read. We need always to ask ourselves: What kinds of messages am I sending with the work I am structuring?*

—Regie Routman,
*Reading Essentials*

As Regie Routman points out, it's easy to get sidetracked by the details of our daily literacy work and lose sight of the big picture: helping our students become thoughtful, skilled readers and writers. For our teaching to be really powerful, we need to be intentional. We need to have a plan. With the increased focus on standardized tests, it is more important than ever to be intentional in our teaching. In this chapter, we will take the initial steps to becoming intentional in our curriculum planning for reading and writing.

# Naming Our Goals for Our Students

I begin by asking you to reflect on these bedrock questions:

- What does it mean to write well?
- What does it mean to read well?

Thinking about these questions will help you discover and define what you are really after when teaching reading and writing. Your yearly, monthly, and daily plans, which we will focus on in later chapters, will all develop from these core goals.

### The Qualities of Good Writers and Readers

Think about a "good" writer you know—a writer who is independent, mature, and strong. It may be yourself or another adult you know. What does a good writer do? What are his or her habits? Take a few minutes to write down your ideas. List the qualities of good writers.

_____

_____

_____

_____

_____

_____

_____

Now consider what it means to be a "good" reader—a reader who is independent, mature, and strong. What does a good adult reader do? What are his or her habits? List the qualities of good readers.

_____

_____

_____

_____

_____

_____

Take a look at your lists. They may include some of my ideas about good writers and readers:

## Good writers

- use writing as a tool for thinking.
- write often.
- have and use skills to craft and revise writing.
- observe the world closely.
- use writing for a variety of purposes.
- enjoy writing and have a sense of themselves as writers.
- take risks.
- read as writers.
- have an awareness of audience and of different genres.

## Good readers

- read for meaning.
- set goals for their reading in terms of length, variety, and time.
- read often and for a variety of purposes.
- use a full range of strategies to help them understand a text.
- are flexible in their use of strategies such as predicting and monitoring for meaning.
- use background experiences and prior knowledge to predict and confirm the text's meaning.
- evaluate what they've read.
- consider themselves readers.
- enjoy and appreciate reading.
- enjoy discussing and sharing reading experiences.

# Becoming Readers and Writers

Irene Fountas and Gay Su Pinnell describe the goals for learning to read and write in their book, *Guiding Readers and Writers, Grades 3–6*. These goals are based on their understanding of what good, strong readers and writers do.

**Learning to read in the fullest sense means developing decoding skills, but it also means much more. It means becoming readers who**

- read voluntarily and often.
- read a wide variety of materials.
- have confidence in themselves as readers.
- present themselves as readers to others.
- read to become informed on a wide range of topics.
- read to improve their lives.
- read to have satisfying and rewarding vicarious experiences.
- read to expand their world beyond the here and now.
- collect books and refer to favorites again and again.
- recommend books to others.
- talk with others about what they read.
- know authors and illustrators, genres, and styles.
- develop preferences and constantly expand them.
- reflect on their reading.
- make connections between and among the things they have read.
- think critically about what they read.

**Learning to write in the fullest sense means more than developing composition and spelling skills. It means becoming writers who**

- write voluntarily and often.
- write in a wide variety of genres.
- have confidence in themselves as writers.
- present themselves as writers to others.
- use writing as a tool for thinking.
- write to communicate on personal and professional levels.
- write to share experiences or information with others.
- are sensitive to other writers, noticing techniques and styles.
- invite comments on, responses to, and critiques of their writing.
- draw on literary knowledge as a resource for their writing.
- use organized sets of information as a resource for their writing.
- explore favorite topics and genres.

As you consider the qualities you listed for good readers and good writers, think about the implications for your classroom practice. If the ultimate goal is for students to grow to be "thoughtful, mature" readers and writers, what needs to happen in your classroom? What needs to happen throughout the intermediate grades to create readers and writers who are capable, confident risk takers, people who read and write for authentic purposes?

If thoughtful, mature readers spend time reading, have we set aside enough time in our daily schedules for students to read? Are we giving our students a chance to try out the strategies we are teaching them? If we think good writers spend time revising their writing, are we giving our students enough time to write and revise or are we doing all the revision for them? Do our students enjoy reading and writing? Do we let them choose their own topics so they feel invested in them? Do they feel like they are part of the "literacy club"? Are they being exposed to a variety of writing genres or are they simply filling in graphic organizers and writing to a pattern?

> *If proficient readers typically read extensively on their own, as the research suggests, it would seem prudent, even scientific, to develop this habit in young readers.*
>
> —Thomas Newkirk

## A Rationale for Reading and Writing Workshop

Often, intermediate teachers ask me why they should teach a reading and writing workshop when their days are already full of reading and writing experiences in the content areas. Feeling the pressure of a demanding, content-rich curriculum—not to mention test preparation— teachers of grades 3–5 tell me that they just don't have time to teach reading and writing in this way. They feel that teaching students to read is the job of primary-grade teachers, while their goal is to teach students to learn content through reading. Similarly, they teach writing as a vehicle for conveying content information.

Yet this approach misses the instructional mark for most students. For example, when teaching is focused on covering curriculum from social studies or science textbooks, the reading material often only meets the needs of one third of the class. The text is too difficult for some, too easy for others. Indeed, in upper elementary grades, students are still learning to read. We cannot expect them to absorb the content they encounter without support and strategies for tackling the variety of challenging texts from which we want them to learn—textbooks, primary sources, Internet sites, newspapers, and so on.

From a reading perspective, the daily workshop model helps all readers become stronger by matching them up to just-right texts, texts that students can and want to read. From a writing perspective, the workshop model helps young writers build strength, stamina, composition skills, and confidence as they cultivate their own ideas and explore different formats for expression. The teachers with whom I work find that focusing on developing readers and writers on a daily basis is truly differentiated instruction at its best. The next few chapters outline the workshop format and content and provide professional resources for learning more about this approach.

## Matching Our Goals to Our Current Practices

Use this next exercise to help you think about how your current practices may or may not be fulfilling each attribute on your "good writers" and "good readers" lists. In the left column of the chart on page 17 write the good reader and writer attributes you listed earlier (along with any others you want to consider from the examples given on pages 13 and 14). Then take some time to think about examples from your current practice that support these attributes and note them in the column on the right. The following example shows how your chart might look.

| Good Writers | Current Examples From My Classroom |
|---|---|
| consider themselves writers. | Students choose their own writing projects during writing workshop, and they bring in projects they are working on at home. |
| write a lot. | I have scheduled a writing workshop in addition to the content-area writing work that students do during the day. |
| use writing for a variety of purposes. | My classroom environment and schedule provide opportunities for students to write for a variety of purposes throughout the day. |
| use writing as a tool for thinking. | I'd like to encourage students to use writing to prepare for literature circle discussions. |

| Good Writers | Current Examples From My Classroom |
|---|---|
|  |  |
|  |  |
|  |  |
|  |  |

| Good Readers | Current Examples From My Classroom |
|---|---|
|  |  |
|  |  |
|  |  |
|  |  |

Be tough on yourself as you reflect on your current practices. For example, if you find yourself jotting down "enjoy reading" in the left column and "create posters or book reports" in the right column, pause and reflect: Does creating a book report and displaying it on a cereal box or filling in a story map poster truly help my students enjoy reading more? Does it advance any of the good-reader goals I have for them? It may be fun and you may have great-looking bulletin boards, but do strong, proficient readers ever report on their reading in this way in the real world?

A third-grade teacher I know has been assigning daily reading-log entries to her students for homework. She recently noticed that some of her most independent and strongest readers had begun to read independently less and less. Parents complained that students who normally read a lot at home were avoiding reading independently. When the teacher took some time to talk to these readers, she discovered that she had inadvertently trained them to associate pleasure reading with meaningless writing activities. Imagine what it was doing to the struggling readers in her room. Wisely, she began assigning brief writing assignments on a limited basis only for authentic reasons such as preparing one's thoughts for a peer book discussion. This kind of writing in response to reading reflects what proficient readers, such as those in a monthly book club, do.

Remember that there is a difference between assigning reading and writing activities and developing readers and writers. Before you can decide how to plan for instruction, you must consider what it really means to develop readers and writers.

In doing this brief exercise, you will tap into the essence of effective planning—to continually articulate the outcomes you want for your students and put them side by side with your teaching practices, to see if what you do in the classroom truly lives up to your goals. Now, let's take a closer look at intentional teaching.

Good readers read voluntarily and often.

# Good Teaching, Effective Test Prep

My colleague Lynn Holcomb, a language arts coordinator in Dobbs Ferry, New York, has been working with teachers of grades 3–5 on how to meet the requirements of standardized tests while still holding true to beliefs about good teaching. Lynn describes part of her work with teachers and students on literature response and corresponding test requirements as follows:

*Although our students were able to discuss their responses with one another in partnerships and book clubs in meaningful ways, they had difficulty responding well to literature in writing. As the testing requirements became more and more demanding, we realized that we needed to teach our students how to respond to literature in a written format—the same way the ELA test requires them to respond to passages. We decided to study how to teach response to literature by reading Janet Angelillo's Writing About Reading in an after-school study group. We also added a two-week Written Response to Literature unit to both our reading and our writing calendars. We studied the types of questions that students were required to answer when responding to passages on the test and found that there were common expectations for all "constructed responses":*

- *answering the exact question asked,*
- *referring back to the passage or passages read (sometimes students must read two passages and answer a question involving both of them),*
- *using evidence from the text to support an idea.*

*Based on what we learned, we developed mini-lessons on how to refer back to particular passages and use evidence in the text when responding to book club or independent books. Students kept response notebooks and used their written work to prepare for book club or partnership discussions as well as for whole-class Read Aloud discussions. Although they were learning how to expand their thinking and articulate their opinions more thoroughly, students were also learning the skills they would need to take the fourth-grade ELA test in January. Once these skills were well developed through Read Aloud, book club, and partnership responses, we made the connection between the ELA tests and written responses for the tests. Now we asked them to respond to questions after reading "test prep" passages, all the while reminding students that they needed to respond to these types of questions in the same way they would when they were preparing for a book club discussion.*

*The transfer to responding to reading passages was much easier for the students this year than in previous years, and we credit this to the difference in our approach to teaching written response to literature.*

# Intentional Teaching

Teachers tell me all the time about new ideas they can't wait to try out. They love the ideas at first, but after a while, the appeal dies out. The teachers become bored and so do the students. There is no energy left. I believe this happens because too often we are not intentional when we choose to do something. We get caught up in themes, holidays, and events while trying to integrate reading and writing into all of the content areas—and we forget to examine whether the actual work will be useful for our developing readers and writers. We decide to study Haiku poetry during a Japan unit, for example, because we need a writing component and thematically, this matches.

While theme-based teaching can be rich and rigorous, it is important to remember that teaching reading and writing is different from using reading and writing to learn content. We need to teach students to use writing and reading to learn content. And we need to be intentional in our planning of reading, writing, and content areas. We can ask students to write research projects during science, using the writing to help

## Know and Apply the Research on Effective Teaching

Students in classrooms with effective teachers become better readers regardless of the approach, program, or materials the teachers use. Researcher Richard Allington cites six common, interactive practices of these effective teachers:

- Their students spend about 50 percent of the day reading and writing; in less effective classrooms, students may spend only 10 percent of the day reading and lots of time on "stuff."
- Their students spend enormous amounts of time reading easy, on-level texts that they can read with fluency, accuracy, and comprehension.
- Well-crafted, explicit demonstrations and explanations are standard practice during all aspects of reading instruction—whole class, small group, individual.
- They promote purposeful, open-ended talk (teacher to student and student to student) that is "more conversational than interrogational."
- The tasks they assign are meaningful and challenging, involve some student choice, and often integrate several content areas (reading, writing, and social studies, for example).
- They evaluate student work more on improvement and effort than on achievement. They prepare rubrics students can use to evaluate their own work. They spend little time preparing for standardized tests.

them learn the content, but we also must continue to focus on teaching the writer during writing workshop, where students choose their own topics.

## Intention in Reading Workshop

The act of reading needs to predominate in the reading workshop. Explicit instruction has to be balanced with lots of time for application. Our plans must reflect this intention.

It's important to think about what students need to learn from each unit or topic in a reading and writing program. If they are learning how to "make connections" in reading, for example, I list my goals for that skill. Then I integrate the goals into my reading workshop. I model making connections during Read Aloud. I look for evidence that students are making connections while conferring during independent reading. My assessment method helps me to notice if students are making connections. I incorporate making-connection strategies into homework and have students practice them in guided reading groups and literature circles. This is very different than choosing a topic to cover or teaching a theme like "friendship" across the disciplines.

## Intention in Writing Workshop

It's the same with writing workshop. We need to consider the components of our program (mini-lessons, independent writing time, materials, "author-share" sessions) and then decide whether or not they support what we are studying. Teaching writing is not magical. It is not easy either. The hardest part is coming to feel that we know what we're doing. Some of us give students activities, topics to write about, or prompts to write from and call that writing workshop. Some of us teach kids a "magic pattern" and call that writing instruction.

Other teachers have gotten the impression that workshop teaching is simply letting kids write and write without worrying about spelling and grammar. They've seen "writing workshops" and don't want to try it because they don't think it provides enough instruction. However, if you are not intentionally teaching the writers during a writing workshop, those writers won't learn about spelling, grammar, or craft. One of the essential components of a writing workshop is teaching. A gimmick or pattern may help us feel like we're doing something, but I find that when students are taught a pattern, all the writing has the same inauthentic tone. Being intentional and "planful" (purposeful in planning) gives us a true sense of confidence. When we feel in control and confident, we're more comfortable allowing for spontaneity and creativity, and our students learn to really write.

# Being a Learner of Teaching

In her book *On Solid Ground*, Sharon Taberski helps us think about teaching with intention in a reading and writing curriculum. Hers is yet another voice reminding us that we need first to be learners of teaching. She asks us to consider these questions:

- Are you using your time well?
- Have you established goals and created the supports that enable you to be successful?
- Are you making connections among all the things you do?
- Does your day make sense for you and your students?

Taberski has spent years learning to think about her teaching systematically. Everything is part of the system, the components of the day, goals for literacy teaching, and the teacher's role. So creating plans for a comprehensive, balanced literacy program and being intentional in our teaching is much more than just deciding what to teach. It's more about naming your goals for the readers and writers in your class and making sure all the components of your program support those goals. It's hard work, but the payoff is huge. Taberski says it best:

*Gone are the days when I leave my classroom exhausted and overwhelmed by countless and often contradictory demands. I'm no longer worn out from "pushing and pulling" children through unconnected activities that others say are good for them. I know what I want to happen and I'm clear about my role in helping children. And I assess my teaching and children's learning continuously, so I can do more of what's working and less of what isn't.*

# Intentional Planning

**P**lanning curriculum based on our goals isn't only about the work we and our students are doing. We must consider all of the components of an effective intermediate classroom:

- assessments
- materials
- room organization
- schedules
- flexible grouping of students

## Assessing Students Intentionally

When I began teaching, I thought of assessment as something that came at the end of a unit, after I had covered a part of the curriculum. I tested students to see if they "got it." However, when my focus shifted from worrying about what I was going to cover to what I noticed the students doing in reading and writing, it became clear what I needed to teach. I didn't need to rely so heavily on the teacher's manuals. I found that I was using materials and not being used by them.

More recently, I joined the teachers at the Roberts Avenue School in Danbury, Connecticut, to study assessment and to develop more-meaningful ways of using it to drive instruction. In the process, we arrived at the following conclusions:

- We always begin with what the child knows.
- We value the process as much as the product.
- We encourage self-assessment.
- We believe assessment should be ongoing, objective, varied, open, honest, reflective, and integrated.

Literacy experts all agree: Assessment that is ongoing—before, during, and after a lesson—is an extremely valuable planning tool. As Richard Allington explains, "When students write, you can see what they need to learn." And when we listen to students read and take careful notes on what they do, we see what they need to learn. Kenneth and Yetta Goodman call this "kid watching." J. Richard Gentry, in his book *The Literacy Map*, reminds us of the importance of working quickly at the beginning of the school year to get to know all the students as individuals. He suggests we start by asking these questions about each student:

- Is the student reading independently?
- On what level is he or she reading?
- What are his or her attitudes about books?
- How is this student coming along as a writer?
- What is he or she passionate about, and how can I cultivate that passion into reading and writing?
- What important spelling work does this student need?

I'd add:

- Does the student consider him- or herself a reader and a writer?

In the classrooms where I work, I encourage teachers to assess each student with questions like these in a written interview format during the first few weeks of school. I also encourage them to administer a running record for each student to find out the reading strategies he or she is using. Writing workshop begins on the very first day of school, with students choosing their own topics. This enables us to learn right away about each student and his or her views about writing. The point is, authentic assessment will drive instruction. Talking to kids about what they know, what they don't know, and what they want to know, will make it possible for you to plan. How do you know what you need to teach unless you find out what your students already know?

*By carefully observing individual students in the course of ongoing classroom activities, we evaluate, reflect, and revise our instructional plans on the basis of what students do. We let students know when they are successful in a learning task and provide the support they need to complete tasks they are yet unable to do on their own. Equally important, kid-watching is a way for us to evaluate ourselves and our teaching.*

*—Mary Browning Schulman and Carleen DaCruz Payne*

## Organizing Notes and Records

I spent many years in my own classroom developing and fine-tuning my assessment practices. I used a wide variety of techniques and record-keeping tools that I recommend to the teachers I advise, including these:

- anecdotal notes
- running records
- student interviews
- family interviews
- observations during reading, spelling, writing, and speaking
- conversations with students (conferences)

I used a three-ring binder for my long-term assessment records, with a tabbed section for each student. In it, I would store anecdotal notes, interview forms, spelling assessments, running-record forms, as well as math assessments and writing samples.

For daily assessment records, I kept a clipboard with a cover sheet that listed the entire class. After each student's name, I'd write the date when I held a conference with him or her. By glancing at the cover sheet, I could quickly see with whom I needed to meet on any given day. Under the cover sheet, I kept a form for each student, on which I listed anecdotal notes and quick running records taken during independent reading and writing. To get a sense of patterns of learning and needs in the class, I would regularly flip through the pages. For instance, if I flipped through the pages and noticed that eight or ten students needed work on punctuation or elaboration in writing, I knew what to focus on for the next mini-lesson in writing workshop.

Daily assessment cover sheet and anecdotal note form.

About once a month or so, I placed each child's forms from the clipboard in his or her section of the assessment binder. That way, I would have everything together when it came time to write evaluations for conferences and report cards.

Many of the teachers with whom I now work use a similar assessment routine. Some use spiral-bound notebooks. Some use cards or sticky labels on which they write notes. Later they affix the labels in a notebook organized by date, subject, or student. I have never seen two teachers use exactly the same record-keeping method.

You, too, will likely modify the forms and routines to fit your own style and needs. The point is to have a comfortable assessment routine and a practical, efficient way to keep track of your assessments so that you can be intentional as you use authentic assessment to drive instruction. Most of all, your notes should be useful to you. What are you curious about? What patterns do you see across your class? What do you need to do next? If you find that you are not rereading your notes, you probably need to take notes differently. You may need to make an adjustment—or several; it takes time to find a system that works. Also, you will find that the type of notes you take will change over time, depending on the unit you are exploring or the time of year.

### Determining Developmental Levels

Gay Su Pinnell and Irene Fountas offer two wonderful charts that outline the growth of readers and writers over time, from kindergarten to grade 6. (See pages 28 and 29.) They list developmental levels at the top of each column, characteristics of readers and writers within each column, and approximate grade levels at the bottom of each column. As such, they encourage us to consider students first instead of grade level. I've included the charts for kindergarten to grade 6 because it's helpful to see from where our intermediate students have come. Also, in every class, there is always a wide range of reading and writing skills; it is not uncommon to find fourth-grade students who are "transitional writers or readers," which are described in the "Grades 2-3" column on the chart. And it's wise to look ahead on the chart for every student— not just readers and writers who are below grade level. You don't want to stop assessing a third grader just because he or she holds all of the "third-grade" characteristics.

Supplies should be labeled, accessible, and centrally located.

Intentional assessment means finding out who our students are, regardless of their grade level. The teachers with whom I work have found charts like these helpful in figuring out where a particular student is and where he or she needs to go next. These charts are also helpful as starting points in matching kids up with appropriately leveled texts.

When we think about assessment, then, we realize there is much more to it than what is mandated by the district two or three times a year for benchmarking purposes. It is also much more than finding out if the students got it at the end of a unit. Assessment must drive instruction.

### *Using Materials Intentionally*

If we want our students to consider themselves readers and writers, we must give them choices about the kinds of materials they use. For example, if we are teaching a poetry unit, it makes sense to offer different shapes and sizes of paper. Students should use real stationery and write real letters during a letter-writing unit. I have heard it said that "the material is the method." Choose wisely. If your goal is to create an environment where reading and writing for authentic purposes will take place, students need access to books and real writing tools, as well as real reasons to read and write.

I once worked in a fourth-grade classroom where a student had brought in a newspaper article that reported on the decline of a type of falcon in the local area. The students were outraged by the fact that a certain common lawn pesticide seemed to be to blame. They developed a campaign to educate the community. Their teacher wisely encouraged this independent project. Groups of students conducted interviews and created educational posters. They wrote articles and advertisements for the newspaper and even held fund-raisers. They really made a difference in their town. All along the way, they used reading and writing for real purposes. The teacher incorporated instruction on spelling, writing, fluency, grammar, and elaboration in the context of writing for a real audience and for their own authentic purposes. The students used that learning because it meant something to them.

Give students the materials that real writers and readers use and give them time to use them. The materials you use will change over time, as your intentions change. Be thoughtful. If you know, for example, that your plan for the next month is to study nonfiction, you can spice up your library with nonfiction material two weeks before you even introduce the unit to your students. Students will discover the materials and notice things to bring to the discussion at the beginning of your study.

Students who come to school with a strong knowledge of stories, genres, and reading strategies are fortunate. Many of them have had exposure to great stories and authentic reasons to read and write. They often have their own books at home and notebooks filled with their own writing. But what about students who aren't so fortunate? Take a few minutes to list ways the materials in your classroom help you support literacy. Consider what you can do to make sure all students have access to and knowledge of how to use the materials in your room independently.

_____

_____

_____

_____

_____

_____

_____

_____

_____

# Building an Effective Reading Process Over Time

| Emergent Readers [Levels A–B] | Early Readers [Levels B–H] | Transitional Readers [Levels H–M] | Self-Extending Readers [Levels M–R] | Advanced Readers [Levels R–Y] |
|---|---|---|---|---|
| • Become aware of print.<br>• Read orally, matching word by word.<br>• Use meaning and language in simple texts.<br>• Hear sounds in words.<br>• Recognize names and some letters.<br>• Use information from pictures.<br>• Connect words with names.<br>• Notice and use spaces between words.<br>• Read orally.<br>• Match one spoken word to one printed word while reading one or two lines of text.<br>• Use spaces and some visual information to check on reading.<br>• Know the names of some alphabet letters.<br>• Know some letter-sound relationships.<br>• Read left to right.<br>• Recognize a few high-frequency words. | • Know names of most alphabet letters and many letter-sound relationships.<br>• Use letter-sound information along with meaning and language to solve words.<br>• Read without pointing.<br>• Read orally and begin to read silently.<br>• Read fluently with phrasing on easy texts; use the punctuation.<br>• Recognize most easy high-frequency words.<br>• Check to be sure reading makes sense, sounds right, looks right.<br>• Check one source of information against another to solve problems.<br>• Use information from pictures as added information while reading print. | • Read silently most of the time.<br>• Have a large core of known words that are recognized automatically.<br>• Use multiple sources of information while reading for meaning.<br>• Integrate sources of information such as letter-sound relationships, meaning, and language structure.<br>• Consistently check to be sure all sources of information fit.<br>• Do not rely on illustrations but notice them to gain additional meaning.<br>• Understand, interpret, and use illustrations in informational texts.<br>• Know how to read differently in some different genres.<br>• Have flexible ways of problem-solving words, including analysis of letter-sound relationships and visual patterns.<br>• Read with phrasing and fluency at appropriate levels. | • Read silently; read fluently when reading aloud.<br>• Use all sources of information flexibly in a smoothly orchestrated way.<br>• Sustain reading over texts with many pages, that require reading over several days or weeks.<br>• Enjoy illustrations and gain additional meaning from them as they interpret texts.<br>• Interpret and use information from a wide variety of visual aids in expository texts.<br>• Analyze words in flexible ways and make excellent attempts at new, multisyllabic words.<br>• Have systems for learning more about the reading process as they read so that they build skills simply by encountering many different kinds of texts with a variety of new words.<br>• Are in a continuous process of building background knowledge and realize that they need to bring their knowledge to their reading.<br>• Become absorbed in books.<br>• Begin to identify with characters in books and see themselves in the events of the stories.<br>• Connect texts with previous texts read. | • Read silently; read fluently when reading aloud.<br>• Effectively use their understandings of how words work; employ a wide range of word-solving strategies, including analogy to known words, word roots, base words, and affixes.<br>• Acquire new vocabulary through reading.<br>• Use reading as a tool for learning in the content areas.<br>• Constantly develop new strategies and new knowledge of texts as they encounter greater variety.<br>• Develop favorite topics and authors that form the basis of lifelong reading preferences.<br>• Actively work to connect texts for greater understanding and finer interpretations of texts.<br>• Consistently go beyond the text to form their own interpretations and apply understandings in other areas.<br>• Sustain interest and understanding over long texts and read over extended periods of time.<br>• Notice and comment on aspects of the writer's craft.<br>• Read to explore themselves as well as philosophical and social issues. |
| *Texts: Simple stories with one–two lines.* | *Texts: Longer books with high-frequency words and supportive illustrations.* | *Texts: Texts with many lines of print; books organized into short chapters; more difficult picture books; wider variety of genres.* | *Texts: Wide reading of a variety of long and short texts; variety of genres.* | *Texts: Wide reading of a variety of genres and for a range of purposes.* |
| **Approximate Grades: K–1** | 1–2 | 2–3 | 3–4 | 4–6 |

# Building an Effective Writing Process Over Time

| Emergent Writers | Early Writers | Transitional Writers | Self-Extending Writers | Advanced Writers |
|---|---|---|---|---|
| • Write name left to right.<br>• Write alphabet letters with increasingly accurate letter formation.<br>• Hear and represent some consonant sounds at the beginning and ends of words.<br>• Use some letter names in the construction of words.<br>• Sometimes use spaces to separate words or attempted words.<br>• Label drawings.<br>• Establish a relationship between print and pictures.<br>• Remember message represented with letters or words.<br>• Write many words phonetically.<br>• Write a few easy words accurately.<br>• Communicate meaning in drawing. | • Write known words fluently.<br>• Write left to write across several lines.<br>• Write 20 to 30 words correctly.<br>• Use letter-sound and visual information to spell words.<br>• Approximate spelling of words, usually with consonant framework and easy-to-hear vowel sounds.<br>• Form almost all letters accurately.<br>• Compose two or three sentences about a single idea.<br>• Begin to notice the author's craft and use techniques in their own writing.<br>• Write about familiar topics and ideas.<br>• Remember messages while spelling words.<br>• Consistently use spacing.<br>• Relate drawings and writing to create a meaningful text.<br>• Reread their writing. | • Spell many words conventionally and make near accurate attempts at many more.<br>• Work on writing over several days to produce longer, more complex texts.<br>• Produce pieces of writing that have dialogue, beginnings, and endings.<br>• Develop ideas to some degree.<br>• Employ a flexible range of strategies to spell words.<br>• Consciously work on their own spelling and writing skills.<br>• Write in a few different genres.<br>• Demonstrate ability to think about ideas while "encoding" written language.<br>• Use basic punctuation and capitalization skills.<br>• Continue to incorporate new understanding about how authors use language to communicate meaning. | • Spell most words quickly without conscious attention to the process.<br>• Proofread to locate their own errors, recognize accurate parts of words, and use references or apply principles to correct words.<br>• Have ways to expand their writing vocabularies.<br>• Understand ways to organize informational writing such as compare/contrast, description, temporal sequence, cause/effect.<br>• Develop a topic and extend a text over many pages.<br>• Develop pieces of writing that have "voice."<br>• Use what they know from reading texts to develop their writing.<br>• Recognize and use many aspects of the writer's craft to improve the quality of their writing.<br>• Write for many different purposes.<br>• Show a growing sense of the audience for their writing.<br>• Critique own writing and offer suggestions to other writers. | • Understand the linguistic and social functions of conventional spelling and produce products that are carefully edited.<br>• Write almost all words quickly and accurately, and fluently.<br>• Use dictionary, thesaurus, computer spell-check, and other text resources; understand organization plans for these resources.<br>• Control a large body of known words that constantly expands.<br>• Demonstrate a large speaking and listening vocabulary as well as knowledge of vocabulary that is used often in written pieces.<br>• Notice many aspects of the writer's craft in texts that they read and apply their knowledge to their own writing.<br>• Critically analyze their own writing and that of others.<br>• Write for a variety of functions—narrative, expressive, informative, and poetic.<br>• Write in various persons and tenses.<br>• Write for different audiences, from known to unknown.<br>• Write about a wide range of topics beyond the present time, known settings, and personal experiences. |
| *Texts: Simple labels and sentences with approximated spelling.* | *Texts: One or more sentences around a single idea on a few pages; some conventionally spelled words.* | *Texts: Longer texts with several ideas; mostly conventional spelling and punctuation; simple sentence structure.* | *Texts: A variety of genres; conventional use of spelling and punctuation; more-complex sentence structure; development of ideas in fiction and nonfiction; use of a variety of ways to organize nonfiction.* | *Texts: A variety of long and short compositions; wide variety of purposes and genres; literary quality in fiction and poetry; variety of ways to organize informational text.* |
| **Approximate Grades: K–1** | 1–2 | 2–3 | 3–4 | 4–6 |

29

# Some Materials for Grades 3–5 Reading and Writing Workshops

- an extensive classroom library with a variety of genres (poetry, nonfiction, picture books, recipes, interactive charts and lists, magazines, etc.) and reading material that represents the range of readers in your room; book-cover displays that invite readers to enjoy the featured books

- reading material that reflects your intended units of study, leveled reading material, and individual baskets or bags for independent reading

- easy reading material

- instructional materials that allow students to practice reading strategies

- challenging material

- a place for young writers to keep their writing over time—perhaps a long-term filing system and folders for short-term work (writer's notebooks)—to encourage revision

- individual spelling resource books in addition to lots of reference charts around the room to promote independence

- writing supplies in a centrally located area—pencil cups on each table for a group to share—fostering the sense of a literate community

- different types of writing tools for different jobs (e.g.: markers for editing)

- computers and printers for publishing work

## A Short List of Magazines for Intermediate Class Libraries

*American Girl* (www.americangirl.com/agmg)

*Boy's Life* (www.boyslife.org)

*Cricket* (www.cricketmag.com)

*Dig* (www.digonsite.com)

*Kids Discover* (www.kidsdiscover.com)

*Muse* (www.cricketmag.com)

*Ranger Rick* (www.rangerick.com)

*Scholastic News* (www.scholasticnews.com)

*Spider* (www.cricketmag.com)

*Sports Illustrated for Kids* (www.sikids.com)

*Time for Kids* (www.timeforkids.com)

To get these materials for your classroom, try requesting gift subscriptions from parents, sharing a subscription with colleagues on your grade level, or asking the librarian for back issues to add to your classroom library.

## Organizing Our Space Intentionally

The way we organize and use our space directly supports or undermines our goals. In her book *In the Company of Children*, Joanne Hindley quotes her friend and colleague Isabelle Beaton:

> *Geography is everything....In my classroom I determine the geography. I can put up barriers to communication or I can set things up to encourage conversation. I can establish lonely islands of I's or I can form communities and provinces of we's. Everyone can have his or her own of each thing or groups can share. All the energy in my room can come from me or I can have constellations of energy. And the geography I put in place will do that for me.*

A carpeted corner of the room where featured books are displayed and charts describing current learning are posted creates a learning-rich area for third graders to gather for whole group focus lessons.

A well-stocked classroom library, organized by book baskets, encourages students to visit and browse often.

Think carefully about how the structure of your room can allow comfortable working space for whole-group, small-group, paired, and individual work activities. In the sample floor plan below, notice the

- large and small spaces for whole- and small-group work.
- areas for group and individual work.
- areas for quiet and noisy activities.
- adequate storage for group and individual items.
- clearly labeled work areas and materials.
- materials organized for easy access.
- classroom library with additional reading materials displayed throughout the room, much like a bookstore.

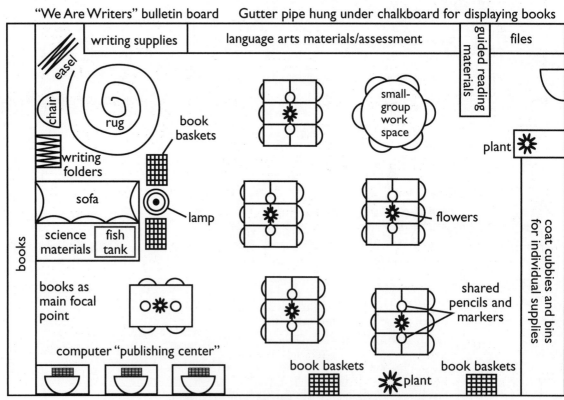

An ideal upper-elementary classroom.

The arrangement of the classroom can facilitate learning and promote literacy. For instance, students write letters when stationery is available. They expand their knowledge of science topics when there are appropriate books at the science table. They explore different genres when there is a range of books in the classroom library. We create this kind of environment by providing

- areas that interest and challenge students, such as an interactive science table.
- a letter-writing station, a listening center, and a poetry center.
- multiple locations for writing tools and reading materials.
- books placed strategically to complement areas of study and to invite browsing (think: bookstore).
- displays that encourage discussion, reading, and writing, such as interactive bulletin boards.
- materials that make it easy to respond to literature, such as sticky-notes, bookmarks, sign-up sheets for book talks, and a bulletin board for recommendations.
- areas for quiet reading.
- areas for group work.

If you take a look inside literacy-rich classrooms like the ones featured in this book, you may notice that they look a little like a living room. If we think back to our beliefs about good readers and writers from earlier in this chapter, it's easy to see why. Where do we as good readers and writers spend time reading and writing? Most likely, we find a comfortable place at home—we don't necessarily go to a desk or an office-like area. I love to visit classrooms that have artwork, lamps, a sofa, a carpet, and plants. These touches set a

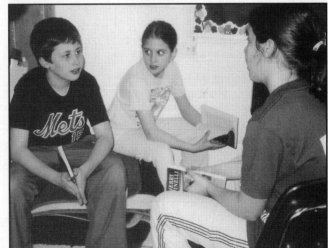

A corner of the classroom with a pile of carpet sample squares provides a comfortable nook for a fifth-grade book club meeting.

tone that respects the literacy learning taking place there. A classroom like that says, "You are welcome to feel comfortable while learning here."

When I asked teacher Kathy Hamilton to describe her ideal room, she described the bookshelves and comfortable seating areas and then, glancing around her current classroom, she admitted, "Everything you don't see here. I really need to think more about my classroom environment and the messages I am sending." She then proceeded to

sketch a map of her current classroom and the changes she planned on making. "Don't you think the library will look great here? It will be the first thing the kids see when they walk in the room. How about a sofa over here?" By considering the intentional use of her classroom space, Kathy saw her room from her students' point of view and created an environment that invited literacy learning in a "real-world" setting.

Take some time now to sketch out your ideal room, using the list on the previous page. Include the following elements:

- whole-group work space and meeting area
- small-group work space
- independent work space
- centrally located materials that support independence
- prominently displayed, easily accessible library
- learning center displays, such as science, writing, and math

Experiment with your room layout. Can you place the furniture so that it meets your intentions for literacy development? If you don't have a room-size carpet, can you make use of carpet samples? (These can be obtained from any carpet store for a minimal fee, sometimes for free.) Does your classroom arrangement have space for whole-group, small-group, and independent work? How are the books displayed? When students enter your room, do they sense that reading and writing are valued? You may consider asking students to help you create the ideal learning space. Ask them what they need to feel comfortable working in their space. I find it helpful to sketch my ideal room layout before moving any furniture.

### Getting Help With Your Room Plan

If you are working with a group of colleagues, visit one another's classrooms to offer feedback and suggestions about room layout, aesthetics, and materials, based on the criteria spelled out in this section.

## Creating Our Schedules Intentionally

Time. There is a finite amount of time in any given school day, any school year. If our schedules match our goals, though, we make the best use of the limited amount of time we have. We give students the time they need to become involved with reading, writing, speaking, and listening.

What does a schedule for workshop teaching look like? I offer an example on page 36 from when I was teaching. (For several other examples, read the professional books listed on page 61.) Your morning schedule (including lunch and special classes) may not allow large, uninterrupted blocks of time for reading and writing, so you'll need to divide up the available time slots in a way that best supports your reading and writing goals.

## Sketch Your Ideal Classroom

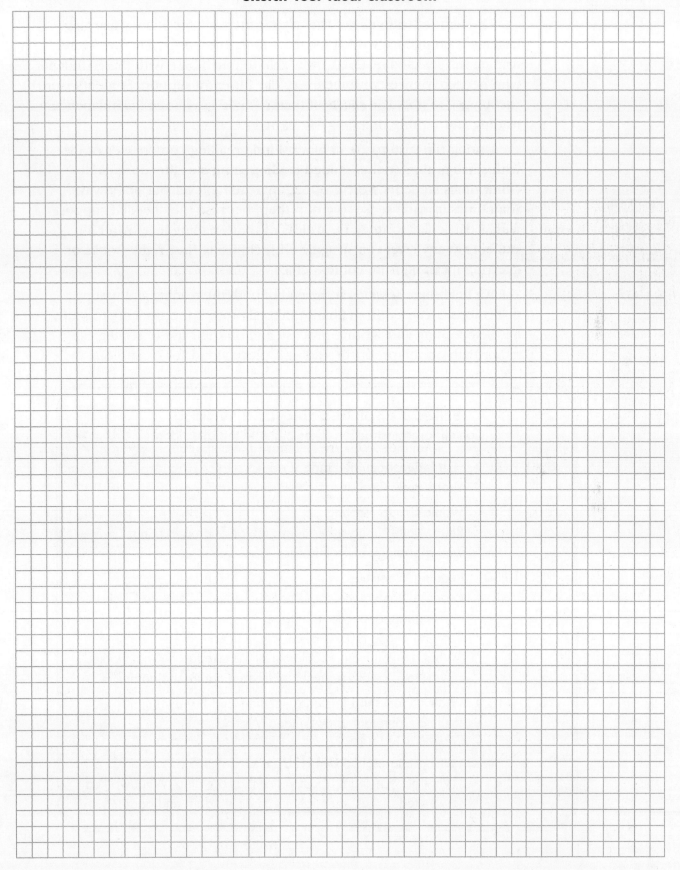

The first few minutes of the day set the tone for literacy learning. Instead of doing busywork, I moved among students while they were reading self-selected material. I was able to touch base with these students who needed to meet with me every day for extra support. Students were encouraged to pursue projects of their own design during the independent reading and writing times.

During the 9:30 to 10:30 block, I held reading conferences or met with small groups (either guided reading groups or literature circles). Other times students were grouped by reading level, but not always. Sometimes it made sense to group them because they needed support with a particular strategy, regardless of their reading level. After all, students at any level can struggle with choosing "just right" books or inferring meaning from context clues.

We held share sessions at the end of both the reading and writing workshops. I learned from Sharon Taberski to ask the students to focus on their reading and writing process, and on their use of strategies, rather than on the product (reading a piece aloud, for example).

## Schedule for Reading and Writing
(Content-area instruction takes place in the afternoon.)

8:40–9:00    **First Independent Reading**
Word-Study Groups

9:00–9:30    **Whole-Group Meeting**
Read Aloud, Shared Reading and/or Shared Writing
with a Strategy or Skill Focus

9:30–10:30    **Reading Workshop**
Reading Conferences or Guided Reading/Literature Circles
    Second Independent Reading
Reading Share (10:20–10:30)
"What did you learn about yourself as a reader? What worked
so well today that you might try to do it again and again?"

10:30–11:20    **Writing Workshop** (includes spelling and handwriting)
Writing Conferences or Guided Writing
Independent Writing
Writing Share (11:10–11:20)
"What did you learn about yourself as a writer? What worked
so well today that you might try to do it again and again?"

Our share sessions began, like Sharon's, with a simple question: "What have you learned about yourself as a reader/writer today?" or "What are your plans for reading/writing?"

This schedule provided time for large-group, small-group, and individual instruction. It offered numerous opportunities for reading to students, reading with students, and reading by students. The reading and writing workshop blocks allowed ample time for students to write, read, confer, share, and listen.

## The Weekly Schedule

I also find it helpful to think of scheduling in terms of a whole week. Diane Snowball, a well-known educator from New Zealand (the country with the highest literacy rate in the world) and author of several literacy books, including *Spelling K–8: Planning and Teaching*, asks us to consider a week of literacy learning from a student's perspective, that contains

- at least four hours of reading fiction and nonfiction texts.

- at least one hour of writing or reading poetry.

- at least four hours of writing, which includes personal narratives as well as content-area writing.

- two or three 20- to 30-minute reading groups with teacher involvement.

- special instruction in physical education and the arts.

- between five and six hours of content-area study in math, science, and social studies.

- between two and three hours of language/word study.

Take some time now to revise your schedule, using the sheet on the next page. Is there a 90- to 180-minute block of time for literacy instruction every day that includes small-group, whole-class, and individual reading and writing instruction? How much time are the students actually spending engaged in real reading during the day? Are there opportunities for independent reading of self-selected materials for a sustained period of time? How much time is there for writing for a variety of purposes and for writing of various types?

# Scheduling Sheet

List the changes you plan to make after reflecting on intentional scheduling. Is there a balance of reading and writing experiences that include reading and writing to students, reading and writing with students, and reading and writing by students? Use this space to work on your ideal schedule.

**Time Block**          **Teaching Activity**

## *Intentional Grouping of Students*

In her book *Great Grouping Strategies: Ways to Formally and Informally Group Students to Maximize Their Social, Emotional and Academic Learning*, Ronit Wrubel reminds us that our planning needs to "take into consideration how the students will perform their tasks, and with whom they'll be working." When we talk about groups in reading and writing workshops, we don't mean groups based on ability or reading level. We group students by what we notice about them as readers and writers, and by how we can best teach them what they need. For example, you may have a small group of students who need support in choosing just-right texts. You may decide to meet with this group several times a week, checking and discussing their book choices for independent reading and moving through your classroom library with them until they are able to make good choices on their own. Or you may have a few students who need help adding details to their writing, so you share a great model text with them as they all revise their narratives. Allow these groups to be flexible—they will change all the time, depending on students' growth and needs. Avoid giving your groups labels, which tend to imply that the group is intended to be long-term and stagnant.

Wrubel goes on to describe and analyze the range of grouping options, beginning with whole class and ending with individual work. Consider these options while planning reading and writing workshops:

- whole class: meeting times, Read Alouds, focus lessons, and share times
- cooperative learning groups: literature groups, learning centers
- small-task, skill-specific, or study groups: guided reading, word study, writing
- informal and lesson- or project-based groups: reading, writing
- socialization and friendships
- partnerships: writing, editing and revision, reading
- individual work

We need to teach our students how to interact within all groups, regardless of their size or makeup. The time you spend modeling, role-playing, and discussing different ways to work together in groups will pay off tenfold in group performance. Your classroom will run more smoothly as groups stay on task and accomplish their goals, allowing you the time and space to confer with small groups and individuals. Remember to listen in on group discussions regularly to hear what

students are saying to one another and to gauge the quality of their rapport. You will gain an understanding of what they know and whether or not your teaching is "sticking."

### *Intentional Teaching Begins With Intentional Planning*

By reflecting on what you're after when teaching reading and writing, you have taken the first steps to becoming intentional in your curriculum planning. By defining your goals for your students, you are better able to analyze your classroom practices (including your assessment, scheduling, and grouping practices), your use of materials, and your classroom organization. Next, we will consider planning the curriculum.

### Creating Curriculum Binders

You will be creating yearly, monthly, and daily plans for your reading and/or writing workshops. These plans will grow directly from the work you've done in this chapter, which is your analysis of your current literacy practices. I will show you how to create yearlong plans and then how to translate those plans into monthly and daily plans. In the end, you will create a document that will be organized and housed in a three-ring curriculum binder. (In fact, you may want to get a jump start on your binder by making photocopies of the schedules, floor plans, and material lists in this chapter, and of the planning forms throughout the book.)

But first, we turn to Chapter 2 and take a closer look at current suggestions for best practices in literacy teaching. As you read, consider your yearlong goals for your students.

## To Do

Photocopy and collect samples of schedules and classroom layouts from Chapter 1 and from respected colleagues to put in your curriculum binder. As you create your plans, you'll refer back to these bottom-line recommendations in order to make sure that you are planning, teaching, and structuring your space intentionally.

# Comprehensive Literacy Teaching
## Best Practices to Consider for Grades 3–5

*Teaching is about loving questions and moving students to search for answers. A great teacher gets excited about these unanswered questions and becomes an example of quest and curiosity. I admire teachers, but if they act like clerks, the students won't get anywhere.*

—Maxine Greene

## Using the New Standards to Guide Our Plans

Data-driven instruction, standards-based teaching, diagnostic teaching, high-stakes assessment . . . they're not just buzzwords. Now more than ever, teachers are feeling the pressure of standardized testing. Some states are even paying teachers bonuses if their students score well on the tests. I hear from teachers all the time that they are feeling frustrated and nervous about planning curriculum.

It seems that our students are spending a lot less time reading and writing in school and a lot more time working on practice drills for state tests. For many teachers and students, joy has been erased from school life.

Before we can begin planning for reading and writing instruction, we need to take a brief look at best practices for grades 3–5. It is important to balance the need for accountability to state mandates with our understanding of our ultimate goal: to create lifelong, life-wide readers and writers. Just because students score well on a standardized test does not mean that they will continue to use reading and writing for meaningful purposes throughout their lives. The teachers with whom I work want to develop good readers and writers who also do well on tests. We have found that if we teach students to read and write well as defined in Chapter 1, we only need to give them some simple test-taking strategies in order for them to perform well on the state exams.

> I highly recommend obtaining a copy of *Reading and Writing Grade by Grade: Primary Literacy Standards.* For ordering information, contact:
>
> National Center on Education and the Economy (NCEE)
> PO Box 10391
> Rochester, NY 14410
> (888) 361-6233
> www.ncee.org

I use an indispensable guide to standards, *Reading and Writing Grade by Grade: Primary Literacy Standards* (New Standards), to guide my literacy work. The New Standards project recommends best practices in literacy teaching for grades K–3 and focuses on using assessment to drive instruction. While an intermediate-grade version is not yet available, teachers in grades 3–5 can learn from the primary standards as well. Ask the reading specialist in your school whether there is a copy available in the professional library and submit an order request for your school if there is not.

When you look closely at the standards, you'll find that the authors do not endorse any one program or method. Instead, the book is a consensus document that represents years of conversation and debate among the nation's leaders in literacy teaching. Many of the experts in the field of literacy (grades K–12) worked together for more than two years (in conjunction with the Learning Research and Development Center at the University of Pittsburgh and the National Center on Education and the Economy) to create a set of standards for primary students in reading and writing. Respected researchers and educators representing both ends of the spectrum of schools of thought on literacy teaching sat together and came up with national standards as a guide for us all. (I would have loved to have been a fly on the wall in one of those meetings!) The end result is a very usable overview document of comprehensive literacy teaching, which can guide us as we plan for the readers and writers in our classroom.

When I use these standards in my work with teachers, I find that I am comforted by the fact that it doesn't represent any one person's point of view. We can concentrate on understanding what everyone agrees upon as the current best practices—the best thinking of our day. True, ten years from now the "experts" may tell us that some of their ideas have changed. I hope so, because that will mean that new research has been conducted and the current best practices will have been improved. That's what today's accepted beliefs are: improvements on old ideas. And with these improved ideas, we strive to do the best we can and try not to worry about changes that may take place in the future.

Think of the field of astronomy. We now have the Hubble telescope. Experts in the field have gained new knowledge about our solar system and they have also come up with new questions: *Is Pluto really a planet*? In literacy, we have "new" (district-adopted) ways of assessing students, such as running records and DRA, and now we have new information about how students read and write. We also have more questions: *How do we use the information from the DRA to create curriculum*?

It's as if by giving these assessments, we have a new way of thinking about how students read and write. We are able to analyze their use of strategies and really teach. As classroom teachers, we are being let in on the "secrets" that reading specialists have known for years. But with this knowledge also comes responsibility—classroom teachers must also play the role of the reading specialist. We need the tools to help us do our job, to help us be intentional. A real plan, thinking about the big picture, will enable us to be intentional.

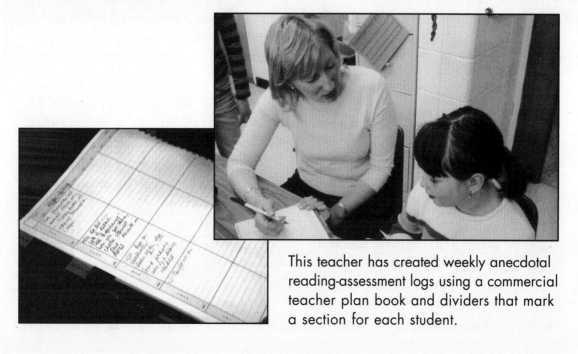

This teacher has created weekly anecdotal reading-assessment logs using a commercial teacher plan book and dividers that mark a section for each student.

The following chart from *Creating Support for Effective Literacy Education* by Constance Weaver, Lorraine Gillmeister-Krause, and Grace Vento-Zogby considers the differences between teaching reading and developing readers, which will aid us as we plan our curriculum and instruction.

| Teaching Reading | Developing Readers |
|---|---|
| **1.** Teacher uses a graded program with an anthology, workbooks and work sheets, and skills tests. | **1.** The teacher uses trade books ("real" books, like the ones found at the library or bookstore) and charts that all can see. Students also have books from which to read independently. |
| **2.** The program determines what will be taught and when. | **2.** The teacher determines what will be taught and when, based on professional knowledge coupled with observation of and interaction with students. |
| **3.** Students are grouped according to alleged ability or grouped according to the results of a one-dimensional tool, such as a standardized test. | **3.** Students needing more help may be grouped for specific instruction, but such grouping is not permanent. |
| **4.** Students' reading is assessed via the basal/anthology publisher's tests. | **4.** Students' reading is assessed with a variety of tools and with attention to strategies used. |

The same thinking can be applied to writing instruction. What is the difference between *teaching writing* and *developing writers*? Are we using assessments at the end of a unit to evaluate the writing the students have produced? Or are we in fact helping to create students who will continue to use writing throughout their own lives for their own purposes? Do you find yourself acting as an evaluator or a coach? When you are discussing a writing assignment with your class, do they ask, "How long does it have to be?" (which shows that they are writing for you and for the grade they hope to receive) or do they ask your opinion on which of two leads would be stronger for the piece (which shows that they consider you a "writing coach" who supports their individual work)? Take some time now to fill in the chart on the following page—and consider your beliefs about developing writers.

# Teaching Writing vs. Developing Writers

Use the reading chart to help you fill in this one about writing.

| **Teaching Writing** | **Developing Writers** |
|---|---|
| 1. _____ | 1. _____ |
| _____ | _____ |
| _____ | _____ |
| _____ | _____ |
| _____ | _____ |
| 2. _____ | 2. _____ |
| _____ | _____ |
| _____ | _____ |
| _____ | _____ |
| _____ | _____ |
| 3. _____ | 3. _____ |
| _____ | _____ |
| _____ | _____ |
| _____ | _____ |
| _____ | _____ |
| 4. _____ | 4. _____ |
| _____ | _____ |
| _____ | _____ |
| _____ | _____ |
| _____ | _____ |

# What Really Matters in Literacy Teaching?

Richard Allington, who studies effective literacy instruction, reminds us to think of the obvious. The completed curriculum binders, which you will create with the help of this book, will help you to stay focused on these truths.

- Students need to read and write a lot.
- They need access to books they can read.
- They need to read and write fluently.
- They need to develop thoughtful literacy.

### Students Need to Read and Write a Lot

Students need to read and write a lot for real purposes. The more they read and write, the better they get. The better they get, the more they like it and the more they will do it. The more they do it, the better they get, and so it goes.

Literacy expert Diane Snowball once shared the results of a study by Anderson, Wilson, and Fielding that correlated the amount of time students spend reading with how they perform on standardized tests. The study found that students who score in the 90th percentile on standardized tests spend an average of about an hour a day or more reading.

> We can't learn to swim without swimming, to write without writing, to sing without singing, or to read without reading. If all we did in the independent reading workshop was to create a structure to ensure that every child spent extended time engaged in reading appropriate texts, we would have supported readers more efficiently and more effectively than we could through any elaborate plan, beautiful ditto sheet, or brilliant lecture.
>
> —Lucy Calkins

Sticky-notes filled with quotes, questions, and reflections provide a helpful tool for upper-elementary readers to develop thoughtful literacy.

## Reading Volume of Fifth-Grade Students and Levels of Achievement

| Achievement percentile | Minutes of reading per day | Words per year |
|---|---|---|
| 90th | 57.4 | 2,357,000 |
| 50th | 12.9 | 610,000 |
| 10th | 1.6 | 51,000 |

A related study shows that the amount of time a student reads in school directly correlates with the amount of time a student reads at home. So, if we want students to be reading a minimum of 60 minutes a day, they need to be reading material on their independent level (95 percent accuracy) for *at least* 30 minutes each day in school. The same could be said for writing.

What is it that students need in order to do well as readers and writers, and consequently, to do well on the standardized tests? They need stamina. They need to be able to interact with text for at least 45 minutes to an hour in one sitting. They need to be able to produce a volume of written material. This kind of stamina is built up over time. A writing workshop (or independent reading time) may start out at the beginning of the year with only 10 minutes of independent writing time. But soon, you'll want to increase the amount of time. Students need practice in reading and writing for longer periods of time.

To do well on standardized tests, students also need to know how to plan their writing and reading. They need to write fluently and with elaboration. They need to be monitoring for meaning and understanding in reading. These skills are best taught in a workshop environment where students are given large blocks of time to interact with print for real purposes.

**To Do**

With a colleague or study group, review your schedules and analyze the amount of time students are engaged in real reading and writing experiences. Do you need to make any changes?

### Students Need Access to Books They Can Read

We need to schedule time in our day for students to read. We also need to use assessments to find out who the readers are in our classrooms. Then we need to make sure we have books, lots of books, in our classroom libraries to represent the range of readers in our rooms. Barbara Peterson's work from years ago about text characteristics and how they support the use of strategies by beginning readers is the basis for all of the current book-leveling guidelines. Publishers are producing book lists and collections with Reading Recovery and guided reading levels. Many teachers use a simple labeling system to level their books: They stick colored dots on the book bindings or covers to mark the different levels. It doesn't really matter whether you use letters or numbers or colors. The point is to know the characteristics of text and how they support young readers.

Marie Clay's Reading Recovery program taught us to look at texts differently. The text characteristics to consider when matching our youngest readers with books at the very emergent levels are these:

- size and style of print
- spacing of text
- placement of text
- level of picture support
- language structure

A fourth grader looks through just-right books—texts he can and wants to read independently.

Other characteristics to consider for readers who are more proficient include the following:

- whether the sentences end on a page or wrap around to the next page
- complexity of plot
- use of humor
- whether each chapter stands alone or the chapters connect to form one big plot
- number of characters
- use of referenced or nonreferenced dialogue
- subject matter

**To Do**

Bring some texts to your next study group meeting or a meeting with a colleague at your grade level. Together, analyze the books in relation to the text characteristics listed here.

## Reading Aloud

Being able to read independently does not diminish the importance of reading in other ways. In fact, when students read leveled books that are within their range for accuracy and fluency, they use only a fraction of the words and ideas they know. Through assisted reading and hearing books read aloud, they are exposed to new vocabulary and concepts that serve as a springboard to the next levels of competence.

If I were to go back into the classroom today as a teacher, the biggest change I would make in my teaching would be to read aloud a lot more. I always read aloud to my students at least two or three times a week. I would make the effort to read even more. One year, I read only one chapter book to my students. Now, I'd make sure that we get through at least a chapter book every two or three weeks. I'd read shorter chapter books that look and feel like the books some of my on-grade-level students can and want to read. I'd also read longer chapter books that more skilled readers can handle. I even recommend that intermediate teachers read aloud more picture books. If you haven't already embraced this practice, try reading picture books on a regular basis to your students in grades 3–5. Some of the best picture books have very sophisticated themes and messages. You'll be surprised at how much they can add to your content area studies as well as to your units of study for reading and writing.

We all know that the students who have been read to regularly at home come to school with a huge advantage. We need to extend that advantage to all of our students. Reading aloud often from a variety of texts (picture books, chapter books, poetry, nonfiction, newspapers, letters, etc.) is probably one of the most important things we can do.

## A Short List of Favorite Read-Aloud Chapter Books

Add some of your favorite Read Alouds to the lists below. Ask your colleagues for a selection of their favorites. You'll want to include such a list in your completed curriculum binder.

Most of these chapter books are a part of a series. I like to read aloud the first book from a series and tell the students that if they liked it, they can find others from the series in the library or bookstore.

| | |
|---|---|
| Janet Taylor Lisle | *The Lost Flower Children* |
| | *The Afternoon of the Elves* |
| | *The Gold Dust Letters* |
| Scholastic | In Their Own Words series—history |
| Mary Pope Osborne | The Magic Tree House series |
| | The Magic Tree House Research Guides |
| Edith Nesbitt | *Five Children and It* (and others) |

_____

_____

_____

## A Short List of Favorite Picture Books for Read Alouds and Shared Reading

| | |
|---|---|
| Patricia MacLachlan | *All the Places to Love* |
| Joseph P. Anthony | *The Dandelion Seed* |
| Julie Brinkloe | *Fireflies* |
| Sherry Garland | *The Lotus Seed* |
| Barbara Cooney | *Miss Rumphius* |
| Jim LaMarche | *The Raft* |
| Thomas Locker | *Sky Tree* |
| Cynthia Rylant | *Whales* |
| Eve Bunting | *The Wednesday Surprise* |

_____

_____

_____

### To Do

Look for a copy of Jim Trelease's *Read Aloud Handbook* in your school library or purchase it. In his beloved, classic guide, Trelease

- explains how reading aloud awakens students' imaginations and improves their language skills.

- shows how to begin reading aloud and which books to choose.

- suggests ways to create reader-friendly home, classroom, and library environments.

- gives tips on luring students away from the television.

- shows how to integrate silent reading with Read-Aloud sessions.

- includes a treasury of more than 1,500 students' books that are great for reading aloud–from picture books to novels.

### Building a Library

Getting books into classroom libraries has become a major priority in the schools where I work. Resourceful teachers bring in books from home, use bonus points from monthly book club orders, and scour tag sales and library book sales for bargains and multiple copies of well-loved standards. Parents donate and give books as gifts, PTAs organize book swaps and fund-raisers to build classroom libraries, and administrators write grants to build classroom libraries. One teacher I know asks parents to "bid" on class-made books and uses the auction money to buy trade books for the classroom library.

A good classroom library offers a wide selection of books organized by genre, series, reading level, favorite characters, and student interests.

Some ways you might acquire library books include

- using book clubs and bonus points.
- working with parents to hold bake sales and auctions.
- making gifts possible.
- asking a local business to adopt the school.
- researching other possible sources of funding such as local and federal governments, charitable organizations, service clubs, parent-teacher organizations, Junior League, Lions Club, or Kiwanis chapters, large companies, local businesses and bookstores, private foundations, family or independent foundations, and individuals.

# Connect Classroom Library to Teaching

Your classroom library should have books that you use to teach from in writer's workshop (touchstone texts), books to support independent reading (about a third of your library should be leveled), books for guided and shared reading, and books from a variety of genres (don't forget magazines and nonfiction). As you consider your library as a whole, sort the books into various categories:

- books that expand students' literary experiences (Ask: Which books offer rich literary experiences and should be reserved to read aloud to students or for interactive Read Aloud?)

- books to support research and inquiry (Ask: Which books are useful for reference or for learning content or for browsing in centers of interest?)
- leveled books to support student's reading development (Ask: Which books are useful for guided reading lessons? For independent reading? For discussion groups?)

Keep these different types of books separate, in different library sections or in labeled baskets.

### Shared Book Rooms

Many schools are creating shared book rooms, where teachers can sign out sets of books to augment their classroom libraries. It makes a lot of sense to share books this way since our goal is to get as many books into the classrooms as we can. It also makes sense when we consider that the books that are appropriate for some students at, say, the beginning of fourth grade, will be appropriate for other students at the end of third grade. Gone are the days when teachers at each grade level had "sacred" books that only they were allowed to teach. If we are truly focusing on developing readers, we shouldn't ask students to read a book that is below their independent reading level simply because it's a grade-level-approved book. In other words, if a child is ready to read *Redwall* in third grade, that child shouldn't be reading it again for instructional purposes in upper grades because it will no longer be on his or her instructional level.

A well-organized, centrally located shared book room.

Our classrooms should be overflowing with books and material that students can and want to read. Keep a wish list at the back of your curriculum binder. Your list can include books you need for your comprehensive literacy program or more poetry books for a writing genre study. Perhaps you could use more level M books for independent reading. If you have a list ready, then when you are given some money (and told that you must spend it by 3 P.M. the same afternoon!) you can use it intentionally. You'll also want to keep lists of what is available in

your school's shared book room. The biggest complaint I hear from literacy specialists is that the books don't always "fly off of the shelves" from the shared book room. Mostly that's because teachers don't have the time to browse and get to know what's there. Make it a priority to request a copy of the book room list and regularly check out books. How helpful it will be when you open your curriculum binder to plan your next unit of study and find a reminder about what is available in your school to support the study. Also, take note of the books you don't use from the shared book room. Was a particular book leveled incorrectly? Leveling books is not an exact science. Some books just don't work for guided reading. Get them out of the shared book room and into the classroom libraries.

## To Do

Take a tour of your classroom library. Are there books for all the types of readers in your room or do you find gaps? If you are working with a study group, tour the libraries in one another's rooms. And if your school has a shared book room, make the effort to find out what's available.

### Students Need to Read and Write Fluently

Our students need lots of practice in reading appropriately leveled material. We know that when a reader struggles with word-by-word reading he or she has difficulty reading sentences in coherent, connected phrases. Too much cognitive effort is deployed at the word and sentence level and little remains for thinking about ideas, emotions and images. The key to fluency (and comprehension), then, is matching students up with books that are leveled for them, based on assessments like the DRA.

Fifth-grade students are given a chance to write daily about topics of their own choice during writing workshop.

Fluency in writing is equally important. The student who is overly concerned with perfect spelling will remain stuck trying to write a word rather than getting a whole idea down first. Over time, with daily practice and direct instruction in writing, students can learn to communicate effectively, informatively, responsively, and even poignantly.

Fluency comes with practice. Giving students lots of time to practice each day will give them a feeling of control over their reading and writing and will also increase their fluency. The key is to know where they are as readers and writers and to match them up with appropriate materials.

As you map out your year in terms of reading and writing curriculum and create your curriculum binders, you'll want to consider when to administer different assessments. There are certain assessments that should be given at the beginning of the year and then repeated at different intervals. Most districts have mandates regarding assessment, but they don't always match up with our vision of good literacy teaching. We'll want to make sure that our assessments are giving us the best information possible in order to inform our instruction. Think intentionally.

## Students Need to Develop Thoughtful Literacy

Reading and writing isn't just about those little black marks on the page. Reading is an interactive process that involves decoding words and constructing meaning. We want students to become active, strategic readers

Book clubs are a great way for students to make choices about what and with whom they will read, in order to deepen their thoughtful responses to reading.

as well as proficient decoders. We need to make sure our students understand what it means to be critical readers. Ellin Keene and Susan Zimmermann, in their book *Mosaic of Thought*, describe how they "want students to develop the habits of mind of avid readers, to succeed in comprehending ever more challenging texts, and to use a wide variety of problem solving strategies to remedy comprehension problems independently." They go on to describe the "proficient reader research," which has confirmed what teachers of reading may have observed in themselves and in their students, namely, that thoughtful, active, proficient readers are metacognitive thinkers; they think about their own process during reading.

Do you model your thought process during writing? How about during Read Aloud? Consider how you can use your shared writing and reading times to model thoughtful literacy.

# Components of a Comprehensive Literacy Program

How can we make sure our students are reading and writing a lot, have access to books they can read, are gaining practice in reading and writing fluently, and are developing thoughtful literacy? A comprehensive literacy program provides these opportunities through Read Aloud, Shared Reading, Independent Reading, Guided Reading, Word Work, Writing Workshop, and Shared Writing—all the components of Reading and Writing Workshop.

### Read Aloud

Research from the National Academy of Education has shown that reading aloud to students is the "single most important activity for building the knowledge required for eventual success in reading" (1985). Reading aloud to students

- familiarizes them with book language and story structure.
- teaches an appreciation of literature.
- provides a model of fluent oral reading.
- expands student's knowledge of various genres and motivates them to read on their own.
- expands and enriches students' vocabularies and background knowledge.
- stimulates discussion.
- improves oral language.
- models good reading behavior for students.

- creates a community of readers through enjoyment and shared knowledge.
- makes complex ideas available to students.
- establishes known texts to use as a basis for writing and other activities through rereading.

Reading aloud to students is particularly valuable for those who are learning English as their second language or who have had limited experiences with print. Instructional assistants, parent volunteers, and older students can also read aloud to small groups or individuals in the classroom. (Fairfax Public Schools, 1995)

## Shared Reading

During shared reading, students observe the teacher reading an enlarged text and are invited to read along. Skills and strategies are practiced in a relaxed environment. Shared reading is a time for direct instruction in a variety of reading strategies. A daily shared reading time for beginning readers may include rereading of familiar texts, introduction of a new text, strategy instruction, and follow-up talk. Because shared reading for beginning readers is usually done with the whole class and teacher support, it encourages students to actively participate.

## Independent Reading

When I was teaching, I scheduled USSR time (Uninterrupted Sustained Silent Reading). Usually it was held during that extra 15 minutes between gym and lunch. Or students could read independently once they finished a scheduled activity. Lucy Calkins, in *The Art of Teaching Reading,* asks us to consider making independent reading central to our reading program. Independent reading should be their "work."

When students are reading independently, we can catch a glimpse of what they are doing in their reading lives. How do we know if what we are teaching during guided reading or shared reading is sticking? We have to give the students a chance to show us what they know. Find out what they know and use that to help them get to what they need to know next. Focus on the positives. During independent reading time, students are reading on their own from a wide range of material. Some reading is from a special collection at their reading level. When I began moving among the students during independent reading to listen to them read and talk about their reading, I began to get a clearer picture of what I needed to teach. I was able to focus on what was going on with book choices. I noticed which strategies a child was using or not using. I noticed whether the child was monitoring for meaning and so on. I got tons of ideas for mini-lessons.

## Independent Reading Tips

Ways to support independent reading include

- creating an attractive, inviting classroom library containing a range of reading materials.

- emphasizing the choice of familiar or easy-to-read books for students to use during independent reading.

- providing time for independent reading.

- establishing clear expectations and guidelines for behavior during independent reading time.

- modeling independent reading behavior.

- introducing new books to the students through book talks.

- conferring with students about their independent reading.

*Fairfax Public Schools, 1995*

## Guided Reading

In guided reading instruction, teachers guide small groups of students who have similar reading processes. Teachers plan guided reading lessons to meet the specific needs of students and carefully choose books that support the purposes of the lesson. Multiple copies of the same book or story are needed. In the guided reading group, the teacher introduces the story, providing students with enough information about a text to do an independent first reading. Unlike shared reading, the teacher does not read the text to the students first. The teacher supports the students as they read the whole text to themselves, making teaching points during and after the reading. Guided reading gives students the opportunity to apply reading strategies to solve problems on unfamiliar texts.

Not all of your students will need a guided reading group. Most often guided reading is used with small groups of three to six students. The formation of guided reading groups should be flexible and change frequently. The teacher observes and supports the child's use of strategies with prompts and questions. A group may consist of students all at the same instructional level working in the same book, or of students who need to work on a particular strategy, in which case they may all be on different levels working in different books. Many of your students may be working in literature response groups with their peers.

### Word Work

Teachers spend 10 to 15 minutes a day focusing on particular vocabulary, spelling, and grammar issues, based on the needs of the class as determined by independent conferences, group work, and reading of students' work. Of course, this is not the only time during the day to focus on these topics. Woven through the entire comprehensive literacy program, teachers have opportunities to help students notice and use spelling and grammar. There is always a focus on vocabulary, spelling, and grammar during writing workshop, shared writing and guided reading lessons. This work may include noticing and charting different patterns or sound-symbol connections. Remember, the focus is on helping students use what they know about words to solve new words. Some of the most successful spelling and grammar lessons I have witnessed involved letting the students define the "rule" by looking at a group of linked words.

### Writing Workshop

Students are engaged in writing a variety of texts on topics of their choice. The teacher guides the process by modeling, providing focus lessons, conferring, and giving students the opportunity to share. Teachers use this workshop format to teach students how to write in different genres and how to improve the quality of their writing. The students have choices within these parameters.

### Independent Writing

Students write on their own, independent of the teacher. This includes notebook writing, self-selected writing, and retellings. Providing plenty of opportunities for students to write independently gives students the chance to use writing for different purposes across the curriculum.

### Shared Writing or Interactive Writing

During Interactive Writing, the students "share the pen" with the teacher as they write together in a group. In Shared Writing, the teacher holds the pen and elicits responses from the students. Shared writing, like shared reading, gives students another chance to interact with print while being supported in an authentic way. You can build on skills and strategies you've been studying in Word Work and Writing Workshop.

## *What are the implications for classroom practice?*

The staff developers at the Teachers College Reading and Writing Project, under the guidance of Lucy Calkins, developed some bottom-line expectations for good literacy instruction.

## Writing Workshop: Bottom-Line Expectations

- Writing workshop happens at least four times a week in every classroom.

- Writing workshop lasts 45 minutes to an hour and includes a mini-lesson, workshop time, and share.

- Students write whole texts that carry their own thinking.

- There is a place to accumulate each child's writing (folders for K–2, notebooks for 3–5).

- Students' writing and books are visible, honored, and accessible around the room/school.

- Teachers read aloud every day from a variety of genres, also talking about each author.

- Teachers offer strategies for initiating and improving writing, noting what they see in students based on their growing knowledge (from rereading notes, articles, professional development, etc.).

- Publication celebrations are scheduled at least six to nine times a year, and the dates are announced early in the year (to staff, administration, parents, and interested community members).

## Reading Workshop: Bottom-Line Expectations

- Each child reads independent-reading books (books he or she can read with 90 percent accuracy) for at least 30 minutes, five times a week in school.

- There are at least 125 books in each classroom that the teacher thinks students can and will want to read.

- About one third of the books in the classroom libraries are leveled.

- Teachers use running records, plus observations and interviews, to match students and books and to develop instructional plans and whole-class goals.

- Teachers help students choose books they can read with accuracy, fluency, and comprehension and help students sustain their reading.

- Students bring books they are working on to and from home and school.

- Phonics skills are used along with contextual cues when students encounter difficulty. (Fifteen minutes of instructional time each day is set aside for whole-class teaching of "chunks," word parts, alternate ways to spell a sound, and other word work skills.)

Teaching reading and writing should not be difficult. Most students seem to read in spite of what we, the adults in their lives, do to them. Frank Smith has said, "Learning is what people do best. If the conditions are right, learning comes easily." The difficult part of teaching reading and writing is sorting out what we really mean by "teaching reading and writing." What is our ultimate goal? How can we set up the "right" conditions so that learning comes easily? Think back to the ultimate goals we defined in Chapter 1.

In this chapter, I have asked you to consider the big picture—what it is we are really after when we are teaching students to read and write. In the next chapters, we will consider how we translate that big picture into a plan for the year.

## To Do

- Evaluate yourself in terms of comprehensive literacy teaching. Look again at the bottom-line practices listed on page 59. How does your program measure up?

- What are your big questions about teaching reading and writing? Discuss them with colleagues.

- Read professional material to find answers to some of those questions.

- Study yourself as a reader and writer with an eye toward how you can use the information to teach your students.

A teacher coaches a fourth grader to visualize as he reads during a reading-strategy conference.

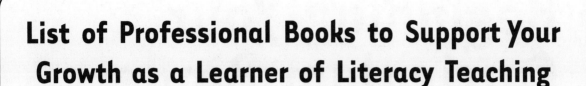

# List of Professional Books to Support Your Growth as a Learner of Literacy Teaching

Fountas & Pinnell

*Matching Readers with Books*
*Guiding Readers and Writers*
*Word Matters*

Lucy Calkins

*The Art of Teaching Writing*
*The Art of Teaching Reading*

Richard Allington

*What Really Matters for Struggling Readers: Designing Research-Based Programs*

Richard Gentry

*The Literacy Map*

Fletcher & Portalupi

*Writing Workshop: The Essential Guide*

Katie Wood Ray

*The Writing Workshop: Working Through the Hard Parts (and They're All Hard Parts)*
*Wondrous Words*

Diane Snowball

*Spelling K–8: Planning and Teaching*

Harvey & Goudvis

*Strategies That Work: Teaching Comprehension to Enhance Understanding*

Keene & Zimmermann

*Mosaic of Thought: Teaching Comprehension in a Reader's Workshop*

Regie Routman

*Reading Essentials*
*Writing Essentials*

National Center for Education and the Economy

*Reading and Writing Grade by Grade (New Standards)*

Frank Smith

*Reading Without Nonsense*

Jeffrey Wilhelm

*Improving Comprehension with Think-Aloud Strategies*

# Chapter 3

# Beginning Your Curriculum Binders
## Using Units of Study to Plan Your Reading and Writing Workshops

*The secret of getting ahead is getting started. The secret of getting started is breaking your complex, overwhelming tasks into small manageable tasks and then starting on the first one.*

—Mark Twain

This chapter helps you break down the task of planning your reading and writing curriculum and start to construct a curriculum binder for each subject. Once you've completed the process, you'll have two comprehensive curriculum documents based on accepted current best practices and the needs of the students you teach. Whether you are working alone or with a colleague, a study group, or all the teachers on your grade level, my hope is that you will find the real value in the process of planning and constructing these binders.

Part II of this book provides a detailed outline showing how to organize your curriculum binders for the year, the month, and the day. The following is a brief overview of the benefits and components of the binders and the organizational concept for planning the year: units of study.

# Benefits of Creating Curriculum Binders

Curriculum binders enable you to

- integrate the required curriculum with current best practices.
- see clearly where you have been and where you are going next in your workshops.
- feel in control of your teaching while letting the students be central to the process.
- integrate new learning from professional reading and staff development workshops into your plans in an intentional manner.
- use your instructional time more intentionally, which will allow more time for independent reading and Read Aloud.
- transport materials easily for off-site planning sessions.
- share your organized plans easily with others.
- see the big picture and focus on your needs for materials, books, and professional development.
- remind yourself to use particular lessons or books again next year and where to find those materials ("borrowed from Ms. Smith").

# Components of Curriculum Binders

A completed curriculum binder contains

- a yearly overview of units of study you plan to carry out in reading or writing workshop.
- a tabbed section for each unit of study (which generally takes about a month) with an overview sheet listing your activities and goals for the unit. Each section contains materials lists, sample focus lessons, overhead transparencies of children's work for teaching, reproducible assessment tools, and articles and chapters from professional books that relate to the unit.
- general sections for reproducible assessment and organizational tools, a materials wish list, overview sheets, bibliographies, and anything else you feel you may need.

As valuable as the completed curriculum binder is, though, it's the process of creating it that helps us most, because we must think about why we do certain things in our classrooms and not just what we do next.

## Yearly Overview Map—Reading

**September**
*Reading with stamina and meaning and losing oneself in a story*
Monitoring for sense
Reading with stamina
Retelling
Envisioning
Synthesizing
Inferring
Empathizing with a character
Using context clues to tackle difficult vocabulary
Using word-attack skills
Reading with fluency
Reading with intonation, expression, phrasing that reflects meaning

**October**
*Readers have ideas about characters*
Envisioning
Predicting
Empathizing with a character
Developing theories
Determining importance
Revising theories about character
Retelling
Citing the text in support of ideas
Understanding cause and effect
Realizing that characters can be complex

**November**
*Nonfiction reading*
Paraphrasing
Summarizing
Identifying ordinate and subordinate ideas
Categorizing
Synthesizing
Activating personal knowledge
Accumulating information on a topic
Inferring
Asking questions
Comparing and contrasting
Understanding cause and effect
Drawing conclusions
Identifying the author's angle
Outlining
Citing text in support of ideas

**December**
*Close reading of short texts, independent reading*
Taking Notes
Rereading
Responding personally
Understanding character motivations
Writing to grow ideas
Monitoring for sense

**January/February**
*Book clubs: Reading with close comprehension*
Envisioning setting
Inferring and interpreting
Reading critically

Rereading with a purpose
Organizing ideas about text to prepare for book talks and writing about reading

**March**
*Book clubs: Inference and interpretation*
Growing and revising theories
Questioning
Inferring and interpreting
Determining importance
Responding personally

**April**
*Content area reading*
Skimming
Determining fact from opinion
Determining importance
Paraphrasing
Reading critically
Developing an idea
Questioning
Taking notes
Summarizing

**May**
*Return to book clubs*

**June**
*Reading projects: Building a reading life*
Reflecting
Assessing
Setting goals
Planning

This overview was designed by teachers from Darien, Connecticut, and is based on work from the Teachers College Reading and Writing Project.

## Getting Started

**Decide who will work on this project.** Will you work on creating a curriculum binder on your own, using this book as your "colleague," or with a partner or a group of teachers?

**Schedule weekly or biweekly meetings.** Planning takes time, so allow for it. I recently heard a radio commercial that said, "Time can mean the difference between a squashed grape and a fine wine." You'll be more likely to stick to the schedule if you can arrange several meetings in advance and mark your calendars in ink.

Some teachers find it helpful to allocate every other grade-level meeting to study and plan for literacy teaching. Other groups schedule a before- or after-school meeting. You might also opt to get together over lunch every week for a period of time. Alternatively, you may want to investigate whether there is a way to get release time to work on this project.

**Limit the number of meetings.** It's easier to commit to, say, six weeks of after-school meetings than to the entire school year. It's also easier to find release-time coverage if there is a definite, limited number of meetings. If you want to continue meeting after the first six weeks, great. But limiting the number of meetings gives people an out if they feel they need it by the end.

**Plan on spreading your work over several months.** Don't try to do the project all at once. Plan on a target date to get everything done and map out a long-term plan. See if you can do this project as part of a district-supported staff development initiative. I've worked with some teachers who were able to use the creation of these curriculum binders as part of their teacher evaluation process. Others have been able to collect continuing-education credits in their states.

**Decide on your focus.** Will you begin by focusing on a reading or a writing curriculum? Reading and writing don't stand alone, and what you focus on in one will certainly overlap with the other. However, I find it more productive and manageable to think of separate workshops when planning for the year. Starting with writing usually works best, especially among teachers without much workshop experience. Once you have established a plan for writing workshop, you can transfer the approach to reading.

## Next Steps

After you have set aside time and decided on a focus for this project, take the following actions:

**Purchase organizational tools.** You'll need some three-ring binders and tabbed divider pages. A three-hole punch will be handy too. Three-ring binders are great because they enable you to add and remove material on an ongoing basis. I like to use the large three-inch size. They're large enough to hold everything you'll want, yet small enough to transport. You'll want one for reading and one for writing.

**Read and start discussing professional materials.** Immerse yourself in the genre of research on literacy teaching. Collect professional reading material and take time to review the latest research on current best practices. I've already recommended the standards put together by the New Standards project. There are also several other great books listed at the end of Chapter 2. Give yourself reading assignments, take notes, and discuss the reading with your group. Keep a reading journal if you are working alone. Find notes from professional development sessions you've attended recently. Reread them. Take notes when you read professional books. Make copies of the bibliographies and charts to which you will want to return. You may also want to take notes during discussions with colleagues. You'll be able to add all these materials to your binders.

**Start collecting articles and notes in your binders.** Don't worry so much about organizing materials yet. You'll be fine-tuning as you go. To start, simply keep writing material in one and reading in the other. Some teachers have found it helpful to keep everything in a basket that is handy to take to and from meetings. The finished curriculum binder will be a reflection of your growth as a literacy practitioner. Ideally, though, it won't ever be really finished. It will be a living document that continues to change and grow.

**Clean out your files.** Just as you would houseclean, get rid of anything you haven't used recently. Do keep any treasures you find: Add to your binders any materials dealing with literacy teaching that you will use. I went through my files recently. I got rid of material that no longer matches my understanding of literacy teaching. But first I had to know what to keep. I had to be up on current professional materials, which is why I urge you to read those materials before you clean.

**As you continue reading this book, make photocopies of charts, forms, lists, and anything else that you feel may be useful.** Keep them in your binders as well. Again, don't worry too much about organizing yet. As you begin to define your curriculum and work with the ideas in Chapters 4–7, it will become clear where to slot the materials so they will be most useful to you.

# Mapping Out Units of Study to Plan a Reading or Writing Workshop

Let's take a closer look at units of study for reading and writing workshops and consider how these units can help us organize and plan.

## Units of Study in a Writing Workshop

Units of study are periods of focus on a particular genre or strategy. In a writing workshop, for example, students may spend time studying poetry, memoir, or craft as a whole class, while also working on individual projects. During shared reading in a reading workshop, the focus may be on the use of a particular strategy such as "preparing for a book discussion." The hard part isn't so much deciding on what to do, but rather when to end one unit of study and move on to another. That's where mapping out the year can help.

Third graders share their work to get feedback from other writers.

Many teachers of both reading and writing have found the words of Isoke Nia from the Teachers College Reading and Writing Project at Columbia University to be infinitely wise when it comes to planning curriculum. Her article from *Primary Voices*, "Units of Study in the Writing Workshop" (August, 1999), which appears on pages 68–80, offers suggestions for planning units of study in a writing workshop. They can be applied when planning units for the reading curriculum, too. Nia explains, clearly and compellingly, the cycle of a unit of study. She also provides helpful tips for choosing "touchstone texts," texts that you can teach from and will return to again and again.

As you read Nia's article, you'll notice that her focus is always on teaching developing writers, even when the class is immersed in a unit of study. Clearly, there's more to teaching writing than giving students a standard pattern with which to write narratives. It is about exposing students to a wide variety of genres and helping them become independent.

While you read, consider how you might use her tips for planning units of study in your own workshops.

# Units of Study in the Writing Workshop

**Isoke Titilayo Nia,** director of research and development, the Reading and Writing Project, Teachers College, Columbia University, New York

In writing workshops across the world, teachers are struggling with the repetitiveness of teaching the writing process. On their walls, they have charts that show the steps of the process in linear or circular shapes. They march their students progressively through these steps, time and time again, like a machine. Faced with the quandary, "What am I to teach?" in the seemingly endless cycle, they reluctantly answer, "I guess I teach how to do each of these steps better one more time or teach random mini-lessons on whatever comes up on a given day." As a study group, we wanted a better answer than that to this curriculum question, and so we searched together for an organizing structure for our writing workshops. We wanted to plan units of study that would carry us across the year with our students.

A unit of study in writing is not unlike a unit of study in science or social studies. It is a line of inquiry—a road of curriculum, a trail of teaching, an excursion of knowing something about writing. It is some big thing that you and your class are digging into over time. For several weeks you plan mini-lessons and lines of inquiry that allow your students to become actively involved in creating the curriculum around the unit of study. If some outside force is requiring you to study something— say, "personal narrative" for the fourth-grade writing test—you turn that requirement into a unit of study on memoir that actively involves students as real writers engaged in inquiry.

## Planning the Year

School years are made of time, and so when we started we looked for ways we might wrap these inquiries around the approximately 180 days of our school year. We imagined the school calendar in increments of time, each lasting approximately three to eight weeks. Next, we had to think about what we might study. As we thought about our teaching and our experiences in writing workshop, we decided there were many possibilities for studies that might help our students grow as writers. We generated the following list of possibilities for units of study:

- genre studies: fiction, memoir, poetry, essay, etc.

- the writing process itself, from idea to publication

- individual parts of the process, such as revision, editing, or gathering in the writing notebook

- living the writerly life

- collaboration (writing in partnerships and other groupings)

- a particular author

- the craft of writing: genre, structure, sound, language system

- difficulty—what are students struggling with?

*Teachers must decide how much they want to prepare their students.*

- using a writer's notebook throughout the process
- stamina in the writing workshop (helping students develop muscles to make writing better)

This list helped us envision what a whole year's worth of study might include. Each of us began the process of making important curricular decisions about what units we would include in our planning for the year and where we would place these units on the time line of our study.

We first considered units of genre studies. The focus of a genre study is on a particular type of writing and its attributes. We began with genre study because it was what we thought we knew (though we would find out we had a lot to learn as we went along). Genre studies seemed available. We had read about them in our mentor books on the teaching of writing by Randy Bomer (1995), Joanne Hindley (1996), and Lucy Calkins (1994), who wrote, "We regard genre studies as fundamental enough to shape our curriculum around them. We find that when an entire class inquires into a genre, it is life-giving" (p. 363). We remembered writing poems and stories as children, and, as avid readers, we knew lots of texts in different genres. So genre studies seemed a logical place to start and they seemed like units of study that could sustain us for much of the year.

## Organizing for Genre Study

We learned through experience that regardless of the type of genre study we were having, the organization of the study was very similar. We organized a study of poetry in much the same way as we organized a study of fiction. The content was different, but the structure of the study was basically the same, as shown in the following structural frame for a genre study.

## Genre Study Steps

Best-Guess Gathering

Immersion

Sifting

Second Immersion

Selecting Touchstone Texts

Touchstone Try-Its

Writing

Reflecting/Assessing

## Best-Guess Gathering

When I get an image of what best-guess gathering looks like in a classroom, I am reminded of the treasure hunts that I participated in at the Brooklyn Museum as a child. I remember getting a clipboard and a short yellow pencil and then being let loose to find a list of treasures. I remember some children lagging behind because the clues on the clipboard didn't seem to be enough, and sometimes the instructors would say more about each clue before they sent us off. But most times it was just us and the clues. It wasn't like the instructors thought the clues were really all we had to go on. They knew we knew more. We were museum students. We were junior members of the museum and were expected to know something about it. Our monthly treasure hunts gave us a sense of ownership, a sense of "this is our museum." When I found the treasure, the museum was mine.

In best-guess gathering, the teacher and the students go into their world on a treasure hunt and bring to the classroom what they think are examples of the genre. Teachers must decide how much they want to say to prepare their students for the hunt. Many teachers do not define the genre at all, choosing instead to allow the definition of the genre to emerge from the gathered texts. They trust that students have in their minds an image of the genre and they want them to use this image to truly make a best guess. Other teachers might choose to say

more—to give their students an image of the genre before they go out to gather....

While most teachers invite their students in on the gathering, this part of the study can be as individual as a single teacher and an evening in the library. It can also be as large as announcements over the loudspeaker to an entire school population: "Class 2-499 is studying poetry. Please help them with their study by placing your favorite poem in the envelope outside their classroom door!" No matter how teachers choose to approach this step, they should wind up with a huge pile of "stuff"—of best-guess genre examples—that have been gathered.

## Immersion

As the material comes into the room, the teacher and students are reading it together, immersing themselves in all their best-guess "stuff." As they choose interesting examples to read, they are beginning to pay attention to the sound and look of the genre and noticing the writing they admire. They are sorting the stuff into piles—categorizing in ways that help them define the genre. I have often asked students at this stage of a genre study to put things in piles that help them say smart things about the genre. I have to trust them to do this. I have to trust that everything they say is important and will somehow push the learning forward.

Around all the sorting and reading there must be a lot of talking. The students will use their talk to create a working definition of the genre as they notice generalities across examples. They will also notice so much more than they would if the definition of the genre had been handed to them in the beginning.

## Sifting

After students have had time (three to four days) to look closely at the pieces of writing, they are ready to begin sifting. This is a process of

> *Students will notice so much more than they would if the definition of the genre had been handed to them in the beginning.*

selecting specific texts that will carry the genre study forward. We usually sift texts out for three reasons:

**1.** The text is not an example of the genre.

**2.** The text is an example of the genre, but it is not like what we will write. Because of such variety within genres, we must make a decision about what kinds of texts we will write. We keep only these kinds in our sifting.

**3.** The text belongs to the genre, and it is like what we will write, but it just isn't good writing. We just don't like it so we take it out. This is also when I'd remove anything that might not be appropriate content for the class to use as a model.

As you are sifting, remember that the world of literature is large. There is no reason for a single piece of literature that is not the best to be included in the study.

## Second Immersion

Again the students need to immerse themselves in the genre, but this time they are looking at pieces that are exactly like the kind of writing they will be doing. This immersion has so much to do with the ears, with getting the sound of the genre inside the students. It is when students begin to look at the details of the pieces of writing. The beautiful beginnings and endings. The pictures that make you want to cry. During this immersion the teacher is looking for a touchstone text for the class, and the students are looking for mentor pieces for themselves. How do they know when they find them? When a piece seems to jump out of someone's small pile and literally scream his or her name followed by the names of all the students in the class, then that student or teacher has selected a touchstone text (see Figure 1).

## Selecting Touchstone Texts

**You have read the text and you love it.**
"You" means the teacher! You love this text so much that you think just by reading it your students will fall instantly in love with it. Your love will be contagious.

**You and your students have talked about the text a lot as readers first.**
No piece of literature was written to be taken apart or dissected. It was written to speak to us and to help us change the lives we lead. Our first response to a piece of literature should be as readers. Talk first and talk well before you begin to dissect any piece of writing for your study.

**You find many things to teach in the text.**
The text feels full—teaching full. You see so much that you can teach using just this one piece of literature.

**You can imagine talking about the text for a very long time.**
Make sure that the text you choose can carry the weight of constant talk and examination.

**Your entire class can have access to the text.**
A touchstone no one can touch won't work. The piece you choose must be short enough to be put on overhead, make photocopies from, or have multiple copies of the book for no more than five or six students to share at a time.

**Your students can read the text independently or with some support.**
Because you are going to invest so much time and talk in this one piece of literature, you don't really need to worry about whether every child can read the text independently. This text is going to come with lots of support.

**The text is a little more sophisticated than the writing of your best students.**
You want every child to have to work to write like this author. Make sure you choose something that will be challenging. Trust the literature and study time to help students meet this challenge.

**The text is written by a writer you trust.**
When your back is up against a wall, have some old standbys to reach for. Have a few authors you know "by heart" and whose work you really trust.

**The text is a good example of writing of a particular kind (genre).**
There are some pieces of writing that are almost textbook examples of the genre. Look for these and save them forever because they so well represent what the genre is all about.

**The text is of the genre that we are studying.**
For first-time genre studies, try to keep the genre "pure"—meaning if you are studying memoir for the first time, you might not include memoir in the form of poetry or song. You might look only at narrative memoir that first time.

**You have read the text and loved it.**
And just in case you forgot, you have read it and fallen so deeply in love with this piece of writing that you feel privileged to use it in teaching. You run into your mini-lessons with joy because you have under your arm one of your favorites. Your love of the text is fuel for your study.

*Figure 1. Characteristics of touchstone texts*

## Touchstone Try-Its

The touchstone text for the class is made available for every student. For several days students will read and talk about the text, discussing anything they notice about the writing. The focus of the inquiry at this point is to try to figure out how the writer went about the writing. Students discuss decisions they think the writers of touchstone texts have made about such things as what to include in plot, or whether to repeat a word for effect, or which punctuation to use. The purpose of this close study and the conversations around it is to help students envision new possibilities for their own writing.

In mini-lessons and conferences, the teacher is asking students to "try it," try out the different writing moves they have noticed professional authors using. The touchstone try-it is safe, even playful. Students try things in notebooks and drafts just to see how they sound. If they like some writing a touchstone author has helped them to do, they may include what they have tried in their actual publications. The try-its especially help students who are reluctant to revise, giving them a range of options to explore during revision. During a conference, a teacher might help a student try a writing move out loud so the student can hear how the writing would sound. The teacher is alert for places in notebooks and drafts where it might make sense to suggest try-its to students.

## Writing

Students write throughout the genre study. They are collecting entries in their notebooks, nurturing seed ideas for projects, playing with touch-stone try-its, publishing pieces for their own reasons, and so on. In the step-by-step structural frame for genre study that I outlined above, the writing step refers to the drafting, revising, and editing of a published piece in the genre under study. The writing time for this is fairly short (usually about six days) because of all the genre study work that has come before it. There is an additional time period for the actual publishing of this piece of work if it is to be presented in a particular way, such as in a class magazine or in an anthology of poetry.

## Reflecting/Assessing

*Whichever assessment tool you use should always lead to more talk among you and your students.*

After any study (genre or otherwise) the teacher and students should spend some time reflecting on and assessing their work. They should look at both their processes and their products. This assessment can be as simple as a narrative—having students answer a question, or several questions, about their work:

- How did going through this study feel?

- What was hard for you?

- What do you think about your finished piece?

Assessment may also be as demanding as a rubric created jointly by teacher and students. The assessment tool that you choose should reflect the sophistication of your students. I try to begin the year with the narrative question assessment, then move to checklists and rubrics, and end my year with a combination of both. Whichever tool you use should always lead to more talk among you and your students. Your goal is not just to have students complete writing projects. You want them to really understand these projects, and you want to use their understandings to revise your teaching.

The beauty of this frame for a genre study is that it can be used to organize so much good teaching in the writing workshop. The driving force behind this kind of study is the principle of immersion, the idea that students and teachers need to be deep readers of whatever kind of writing they are learning to do. And equally beautiful is the fact that you can be a learner alongside your students. Beginning a study means trusting the learner part of you. You don't need to know everything there is to know about a genre to do a genre study with your students. It is good to have some background knowledge—which you can acquire by reading examples of the genre, books by writers about writing, and books on the teaching of writing—but the best knowledge comes from active involvement in the study with your class.

## Benefits of Study in the Classroom

Units of study are essential to the writing workshop because without them, what is the work of the workshop on a day-to-day basis? Like a learning map you and your students chart together, your studies create a year's worth of curriculum for the workshop that exposes students to new possibilities as writers.

Units of study help to set the pace for your workshop. They add quality and consistency that both students and teachers need in a workshop setting. When study is valued and arranged with skill and care in a school year, a teacher can both expose her students to many genres and have them become experts in a few. When units of study are planned around writing issues other than genre, students are exposed to a wide range of helpful curriculum for their writing lives. Smaller studies (mini-inquiries) of one week or so can be carefully placed between longer studies when they are necessary to meet student needs. These small studies create a sense of continuity in the work.

Many teachers have found it useful to develop a calendar for units of study during the year.... This calendar becomes public knowledge. It

*Sharing with our students this sort of "calendar approach" to planning for the writing workshop has raised both the production level and the quality of students' writing.*

is the learning map that we and our students will use. Publication dates are spread out liberally across the calendar to insure that we will publish often and to give us something to live toward in our studies. This is the quality that we strive for in our work together: planfulness. It is something like how we live our social lives. We plan a social calendar with specific dates and occasions, but we always make sure we leave room for the unexpected—the last-minute tickets to a great play or the dinner invitation to the new restaurant in town.

Teachers have to think of curriculum calendars in much the same way: We learned that we cannot map out the whole year in August. We learned that to live toward study meant we had to plan several times a year. We had to look at our calendars and our students often and reshape our plans. We learned to trust our August thinking and our November thinking and to let one nourish the other. A part of that learning was to accept that we couldn't really know what our whole calendar would look like until we got to June. It wasn't that we weren't thinking about June much earlier in the year. We just realized that we had to remain open to the possibilities that June might bring.

We also learned to take time (in August and at several points during the school year) to follow these lines of thinking:

- Can I imagine how I'd like the work to go?

- What would I like my students to get from a study?

- Why am I tackling this hard work?

- Can I imagine a time span?

- What are the structures I need to exist in my classroom to make this type of learning possible? How can we get them in?

- How important are the writing notebooks going to be?

- What supplies and literature need to exist in this classroom to make our work possible, and where or how are we going to acquire them?

- What lessons will I need to teach? (Leave room for some you can't imagine yet. Pay close attention to what is happening in your class. Take good notes. Study your conferences. THEN, ask yourself again, "What lessons will I need to teach?")

- With whom will I share this learning journey? (Don't travel alone. It's easier with a friend by your side.)

- We reflected on these questions periodically as a group and as individuals. They helped us know what needed to come next on our planful journey through the curriculum year.

## Raising the Level of Work

We have found that sharing with our students this sort of "calendar approach" to planning for the writing workshop—setting publication dates and making clear what will be studied—has raised both the production level and the quality of writing our students produce. The predictable immersion part of any study of writing helps students learn to read like writers. Over time, reading like writers through thoughtful, well-planned units of study helps students develop an excellent sense of what good writing is so that they can identify and emulate it wherever they find it in the world.

Units of study in the writing workshop also allow students to discover the kinds of writers they are. The child that loves poetry will shine during the poetry study and cringe (perhaps) during the nonfiction genre study but will have many spaces in between to write in the genre that she or he wishes. The beauty of genre study is that it never removes a child's right to choose a topic. Though students may gather to study a very particular kind of writing, they are always writing about topics they have chosen themselves. The studies strengthen their sense of craft and help them envision all the possibilities that exist for their ideas.

## Note

All of the writers included in this issue are members of a Writing Leadership Group within the Teachers College Reading and Writing Project, Columbia University, Leadership Project. This group is led by Isoke Titilayo Nia and funded by a grant written by the projects director, Lucy Calkins, from Morgan Guaranty Trust Company of New York.

## References

Bomer, R. (1995). *Time for meaning: Crafting literate lives in middle and high school.* Portsmouth, NH: Heinemann.

Calkins, L. (1994). *The art of teaching writing.* Portsmouth, NH: Heinemann.

Hindley, J. (1996). *In the company of children.* Portland, ME: Stenhouse.

# Units of Study in a Reading Workshop

Isoke's Nia's article helps us think about possibilities for studies that help our students grow as writers. But how do we translate her thinking into units of study for a reading workshop? The teachers with whom I have worked have found several sources for ideas about units of study in a reading workshop. For instance, let's consider proficient reader research by Pearce et al., as cited by Keene and Zimmerman (1997). Proficient readers

- search for connections between what they know and the new information they encounter in the texts they read.
- ask questions of themselves, the authors they encounter, and the texts they read.
- draw inferences during and after reading.
- distinguish important from less important ideas in text.
- are adept at synthesizing information within and across texts and reading experiences.
- repair faulty comprehension.
- monitor the adequacy of their understanding.

I would add:

- Proficient readers visualize and create images with the different senses to better understand what they read.

## Tips for Strategy Instruction

According to Stephanie Harvey and Anne Goudvis, authors of *Strategies That Work*, teaching students to read strategically means we show them how to construct meaning when they read. Comprehension strategy instruction is most effective when teachers

- model their use of the strategy repeatedly over time.
- show students their thinking when reading, and articulate how that thinking helps them better understand what they read.
- discuss how the strategy helps readers make meaning.
- make connections between the new strategy and what the reader already knows.
- respond in writing by coding the text according to a particular strategy (once kids are reading on their own).

### *Possible Topics for Units of Study*

The next section describes some possible units of study for Reading Workshop. I've clustered the units into two categories: *Habits of Good Readers* and *Strategies of Good Readers*.

## Habits of Good Readers

Some of the following may be mini-units, which require a one- or two-week focus. The time you spend will depend on how experienced your students are with the workshop format and your goals for developing readers.

### Thinking of Ourselves as Readers

Do your students consider themselves readers? Do you consider them readers? If we want them to develop the habits of good readers, it's important to build their identities as readers early on. What types of focus lessons can you envision that would help support their identity as readers? As your students begin to name the qualities they want to emulate as readers, create a chart to remind the class of their ideas.

---

**We're the Kind of Readers Who...**

Like to get books for presents

Read every day

Like to read books in a series

Enjoy mysteries

Like to talk about books

Read to find out more about something

Have piles or lists of books "on deck" to read next (We make plans.)

Share recommendations with each other

Like to talk about what we are reading

---

### Planning Our Reading Lives

We can show students that good readers plan their reading lives and have goals for themselves as readers. Focus lessons may cover "planfulness." You may ask students to share their plans for the next reading session during the focus lesson or share time. ("I plan on reading all of the books from this series," or "I plan on finding other books by this author.") A simple, yet powerful, lesson would be to ask students to

choose books for future reading. This is what strong readers do all the time, and by asking our students to be intentional in their reading plans, we are teaching to our goal of developing lifelong readers.

### CHOOSING BOOKS AND BOOK ORIENTATION

Can our students choose books that are just right for them? What does a just-right book feel like? Often I tell students that finding a just-right book will help them grow as readers by allowing them to use their "reading muscles" without exhausting themselves. I explain that it's like riding a bike. If you choose a book that's too hard, it may be like riding a bike up a really steep hill. Sure, you'd be using your muscles, but you would probably also be straining so hard and focusing your eyes so narrowly that you'd miss most of the scenery.

On the other hand, if you always choose a book that's too easy, it's like coasting downhill on a bike. You don't use your muscles so you're not growing as a reader, and you go too fast to enjoy the scenery. (Note that there are times when we want students to be reading old favorites that are really easy, just not all the time.) A just-right book, like a just-right bike ride with some small hills, allows you to exercise your reading muscles while you enjoy the ride and appreciate the scenery.

Spend some time thinking about how you can support independent book choice in your room. Think leveled library. You need books that all of the readers in your room can and want to read. Don't discount peer book recommendations. Give your students an opportunity to refer books to each other (a binder, bulletin board, book talks).

Book choice also involves knowing the type of reader you are and which types of books you like. Students should be able to describe how they choose what to read and also what they do when they begin reading a new book. This is what we mean by "book orientation." Strong readers usually flip through a book before they begin. They may read the back cover or dust jacket flaps. They may think about other books they've read by the author, or other books on the same topic. Good readers usually begin reading with some questions in mind. Make this explicit to your students.

### GROWING IDEAS AND CREATING MEANING BY TALKING ABOUT BOOKS

During a mini-lesson on "smart talk," a teacher guides students to make connections with the book she is reading aloud to cultivate better book discussions.

Independent reading is rarely truly independent. Reading can be a very social activity. Even mature readers are constantly in dialogue before, during, and after they read. When I finish a book, I'll often pass it along

to my mother or sister-in-law. I love to talk about a good book with someone else who has read it. Even when I'm reading a book I don't want to share, I am still having a conversation with the characters ("Don't open that door!") or with the author ("Now, how could you kill off that character?").

We want students to know that good readers instinctively talk about books to "grow" ideas and meaning. We want them to share and talk about books with one another in natural ways. We want them to notice the ways in which they may already be talking about books.

How do we make this happen in a unit of study? We can invite mature readers into the class to be interviewed about their social reading lives. We can ask our students to interview someone at home. We can model our own social reading lives: "I just finished a book that my sister gave me. I called her last night, and we talked for an hour about it. Don't you just love to talk about books to friends? What can we do in our classroom to make it easier to talk about reading?" Our students will amaze us with what they come up with.

Encourage discussion outside of the classroom, too. My daughter recently formed a summer reading book club. She and her friends read the same book and then get together in her treehouse to discuss it. They have discovered that it's helpful to mark interesting pages with sticky-notes to facilitate their talks. And it works—their book discussions last a long time. Good readers love to talk about books.

During a mini-lesson on "smart talk," a teacher guides students to make connections with the book she is reading aloud to cultivate better book discussions.

84

### READING ACROSS GENRES AND TEXT TYPES

Good readers use strategies flexibly, across different genres and different kinds of texts. For a unit of study, you may include these:

- poetry
- ABC books
- old favorites
- mystery
- fiction
- fantasy
- book reviews
- nonfiction
- newspapers/journalism

Be careful not to spend too much time in any one genre. One fourth-grade teacher found out the hard way that too much of a good thing is never good. Her students loved nonfiction until they had to spend six weeks reading and rereading the same books because their teacher wanted to "cover everything" and do every nonfiction mini-lesson she could think of. The kids quickly grew bored and stopped reading independently because they equated reading with having to fill in graphic organizers. The point is to focus on how the use of strategies changes depending on what you are reading.

## Strategies of Good Readers

### Using Strategies to Figure Out Words

To figure out unfamiliar words, good readers use a variety of strategies, including using initial consonants and looking ahead to the end of the word, chunking, using picture clues, thinking about what would make sense, integrating strategy use, and focusing on prefixes and suffixes. These are just some of the skills you may teach in a unit of study. Consider what skills will benefit your readers most and focus on those. You'll want to revisit these strategies regularly until they become a standard part of students' strategy toolboxes.

### MONITORING FOR UNDERSTANDING

Do our students recognize when what they are reading doesn't make sense? Are they reading with an ear toward understanding, making sure it sounds right, or are they simply word calling, what I call "mechanical reading"? When I was a reading teacher, I often worked with struggling readers in grades 3–5. They had been "successful" readers

in the primary grades because they could sound out all the words. But because they weren't reading for meaning, they ended up having real trouble in the intermediate grades.

We want students to listen as they read to make sure what they say makes sense both grammatically, from what they know about their spoken language, and semantically, from what they know about what they've read so far. Students need to be consistently monitoring for understanding before they can successfully use some of the higher-level reading-response strategies. We can make sure they understand how to monitor for meaning by thinking aloud to model our own process during Read Alouds and shared reading, by conferring with students during guided reading and independent reading, and by inviting students to share their own monitoring processes during share time in Reading Workshop.

### Making Connections

By focusing on making connections, we help students see what mature readers do subconsciously. Harvey and Goudvis teach students to categorize and code their connections, "That reminds me of . . ." or "That's like the other story we read," in such a way as to be able to analyze and discuss them.

- **Text to self:** Does this text relate to me?
- **Text to text:** Does this text relate to another text I know?
- **Text to world:** Does this text relate to something going on in the world?

Harvey and Goudvis encourage students to share their connections in natural ways: "That's how I felt when my best friend moved away," or "That book ends like the other book by Gary Paulsen I just read."

Often teachers list on a chart the connections students make during a shared reading session. Then they evaluate the connections, labeling them "thick" or "thin." Thick connections support our understanding of the text: "I can understand how the character feels because I was new to school this year," for example. However, a comment such as "I love pink nail polish too" about a passage in *The Sisterhood of the Traveling Pants* is not as thick. Thin connections aren't substantial; they don't take our conversations very far.

### Questioning

Good readers ask questions before ("I wonder why one of the characters is called Crazy Lady—the title of this book?"), during ("Why does the author keep flashing back to last year?"), and after reading ("I wonder how this story would have changed if it had been told by a different character?").

Some questions can be answered by reading the text. Some cannot. Teachers can model questioning while thinking out loud during Read Alouds and shared reading, as well as during individual conferences. We can chart questions while we're reading and later go back to see which have been answered. Answers to some questions can be found by rereading text. But some cannot. They must be inferred. I've found that the best questioning leads to inferential thinking.

### VISUALIZING/INFERRING

Creating pictures in our mind helps us understand what we are reading, fill in missing information, and build meaning. When we visualize, we combine the author's words with our own background knowledge.

When we infer, we use clues to draw conclusions about something that has happened or will happen. Inferences are different than predictions—predictions can be confirmed after reading, yet inferences generally can't.

It's difficult to describe inferring to students. We can do lessons where we make facial expressions and ask students to infer what we are thinking. We can tell them that we need to "read between the lines." But unless we can find some great examples of writing that makes a reader infer, it's difficult to explain. You may try something like this. One teacher I know used Norman Rockwell prints to help her students understand what it means to infer. After looking at a print, they made comments like "the girl in the picture must be in trouble." "How do you know?" or "What makes you think so?" the teacher would ask.

### DETERMINING IMPORTANCE

Making meaning requires the reader to determine what is important. Readers have to decide what's relevant and ignore other kinds of information. This isn't learned by filling in work sheets. Readers who are given a chance to question and comment during reading begin to know instinctively what is important.

While working with some third graders who were reading *Marvin Redpost: Alone in His Teacher's House* by Louis Sachar, a colleague noticed that the students' comprehension was negatively influenced because they decided to refer back to nonimportant information. Sometimes, students who seem to be getting it can get off track, and we won't know that unless we are checking in with them. Their predictions can lead them on the wrong line of thinking. In the beginning of *Alone in His Teacher's House*, the characters talk about a substitute teacher and how they'd like to trick her by switching roles in the class. It is just briefly mentioned, and the characters never switch roles—in fact, it's never mentioned again.

However, some of the third graders in the discussion group continued to believe that the kids would be trying to play a trick on the substitute. This unimportant detail took their predictions way off track, and their comprehension of the entire book suffered because of it.

### SYNTHESIZING

Good readers think about what they read and stop every now and then to merge new information with their existing knowledge. In units of study, we can teach students to view the end of a page or passage as a time to stop and think about what they are reading. Some of our readers spend so much time trying to figure out the words or get through the text, they forget to take some time to digest the parts of what they are reading to construct meaning.

Some intermediate teachers have discovered the value of using book discussion groups in their classroom. When students have to prepare to discuss their reading with friends, they read differently. Simply asking students to read some, stop and think about what is happening, jot down an idea or two on a sticky-note, and then read some more, will help them begin to understand the importance of synthesizing. Ask students to be explicit when thinking, "What am I learning here?"

# Your Plans Will Change and Grow

The first part of this book has been about why we should plan intentionally for literacy instruction. When I lead workshops for teachers, I often begin by asking what their "big questions" are about teaching reading and writing. I want to know what they hope to have answered by coming to the workshop. Doing so gives me a sense of who my audience is (i.e., using assessment to drive instruction) and helps me decide what information will meet their needs. It also gives the participants a sense of ownership. In the end, we always end up with more questions and implications for further study. In fact, leading a workshop reminds me of writing a dissertation. It's freeing to realize I don't have to come up with all the answers. The best workshops and dissertations end with questions for future study.

So make your curriculum plans to the best of your ability today. The plans will change. You will grow. Your district mandates may change. Your administration may change. The students in your class will change this year and every year. A plan is always growing.

As I said so many times to my builder during my house renovation, "Might as well, while we're at it." I wouldn't have the great arched hallway

in my dining room with the terrific view if I had stuck rigidly to the architect's original plan. He was the expert, but I live in my house. I see the view every day and I know my family and how we use our space. Yes, you may be told by the experts (for example, textbooks, teacher's manuals, or district mandates) what to do. But you are the one living in your classroom with your students.

I find this entry in the *Dictionary of Word Origins* interesting: "Plan: a flat representation on a flat surface. Etymologically—a design that has been 'planted' on the ground. Originally referred to the laying out of the ground plan of a building."

Just as an architect's plan doesn't represent the life that happens within the building, your curriculum plan doesn't represent the life within your classroom, the joys and sorrows which take place within the community. The rooms' shapes, the decor, and the way the light comes in the window all have an effect on what goes on inside a house, just as a unit of study shapes what is going on in the classroom. It boils down to finding balance between the plan and the action, the day-to-day living.

As you plan your year and start to gain a sense of control over literacy teaching, remember to give yourself time. Also, the final document will never be truly finished. You can always revise and change it as you go. When we're intentional, we feel in control, and when we feel in control, we like what we're doing, and if we like what we're doing, we'll do it more, and the more we do it, the more intentional we'll be, and so it goes. . . .

Of course, it's our students who reap the benefits. If we are intentional in creating the best possible learning experiences for them, they will feel more in control of their reading and writing, which will cause them to like it more, and if they like it, they'll do more, and if they do more, they'll continue to grow, and, of course, the more they grow, the more they'll like it, and so it goes for them, too.

## Stages in Planning a Curriculum

**1.** Make time to plan. (Chapter 3)

**2.** Define "getting the job done" (vision, goals, and roles). (Chapters 1 and 2)

**3.** Map out the year of units of study in each workshop. (Chapter 4)

**4.** Plan each unit of study, keeping in mind workshop components. (Chapter 5)

**5.** Translate units of study into weekly and daily plans. (Chapter 6)

**6.** Reflect at the end of each unit, make changes, and plan ahead. (Chapter 7)

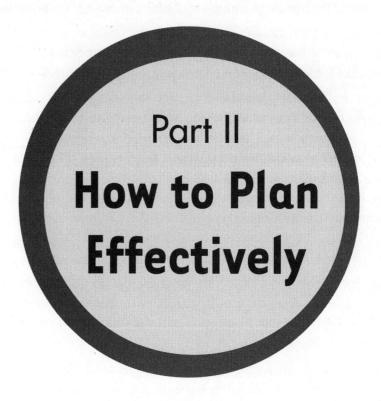

Part II

# How to Plan Effectively

# Chapter 4

# The Big Picture
## Creating the Yearlong Plan

*Like a learning map you and your students chart together, your studies create a year's worth of curriculum for the workshop that exposes students to new possibilities as writers [and readers].*

—Isoke Nia

Once you've defined your goals, started gathering materials, and given some thought to units of study, it's time to organize your curriculum and put together your binders. Begin by mapping out the year in monthlong units of study (roughly ten months of school, ten units of study). Be sure to account for the fact that some units will take less than a month to complete, while others may take slightly longer. Get your binders ready by creating a section and tab for each unit of study. Here are some other sections to consider adding:

- Yearly Overview
- Supplies/Book Wish List
- Spelling/Word Work Materials

- Blackline Masters
- Bibliographies
- Assessment/Conferring Tools

You may decide to start with your writing curriculum first, as the teachers at Roberts Avenue School and Stillmeadow School did. Or, like the teachers from Tracey School and from District 6 in Connecticut, you may decide that you want to tackle reading first. I suggest setting up both binders simultaneously, but focusing on organizing one to start.

# Steps in Putting Together Your Curriculum Binder

The first step is to draw up a big-picture plan for your year. What makes sense for your grade at the beginning of the school year, the middle, and the end? You may want to begin Writing Workshop by studying purposes for writing, the importance of creating community, and self-selecting writing topics. What kinds of school-wide projects will you have to consider? The teachers at Stillmeadow School and Roberts Avenue School must plan for Read Across America Day in the spring. Will your school celebrate National Poetry Month? It is helpful to consider the school year in terms of ten months of three- to eight-week cycles.

But before deciding when to teach, you'll have to decide *what* to teach. Let's start with writing and move to reading later in the chapter.

### Identifying and Scheduling Units for the Writing Curriculum

In *The Writing Workshop: Working Through the Hard Parts (And They're All Hard Parts)*, Katie Wood Ray offers these questions to help us choose what to include in our writing curriculum:

- What are my strengths as a teacher of writing?
- What have my students studied before in writing?
- What are my students interested in? What do they want to know as writers?
- What are my colleagues studying in their writing workshops?
- What resources do I have?
- For what kind of writing will my students be held accountable?

What are the topics/units of study in writing you can imagine studying with your class? Think in terms of genres (memoir, poetry, etc.) and topics (like craft or revision). Create your list here.

_____

_____

_____

_____

_____

_____

_____

_____

_____

_____

After considering these and other questions, Julie Droller, the language arts coordinator in Darien, Connecticut, worked with the faculty and produced this list of topics to start with:

- sense of self as a writer
- topic choice
- building a community of writers
- writer's craft/author study
- poetry
- literary essays
- standardized test preparation
- writing in the content areas
- planning for writing lives outside of school

Other topics to consider:

- personal narrative
- the reading-writing connection
- memoir
- revision
- editing

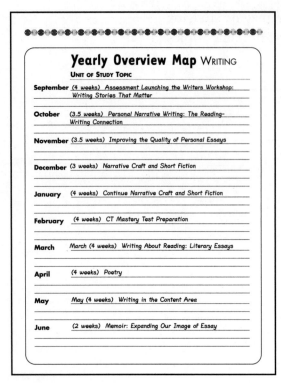

**Yearly Overview Map** WRITING

UNIT OF STUDY TOPIC

**September** *(4 weeks) Assessment Launching the Writers Workshop: Writing Stories That Matter*

**October** *(3.5 weeks) Personal Narrative Writing: The Reading-Writing Connection*

**November** *(3.5 weeks) Improving the Quality of Personal Essays*

**December** *(3 weeks) Narrative Craft and Short Fiction*

**January** *(4 weeks) Continue Narrative Craft and Short Fiction*

**February** *(4 weeks) CT Mastery Test Preparation*

**March** *March (4 weeks) Writing About Reading: Literary Essays*

**April** *(4 weeks) Poetry*

**May** *May (4 weeks) Writing in the Content Area*

**June** *(2 weeks) Memoir: Expanding Our Image of Essay*

Fourth-grade teachers in Darien, Connecticut, developed this plan.

Use the Yearly Overview Map on page 95 to begin mapping out your curriculum. Once you have a list of topics, decide when to teach each unit. You will need your official school calendar to plan for the year. Determine the following: What will be the focus for the beginning of the year? Do you and your colleagues plan on doing any units together?

It makes sense to study certain topics at certain times of the year. For instance, a good unit for the beginning of the year may focus on building a community of readers and writers where students write (individually and in a group) about their reading and writing lives. You'll probably want to leave some spaces open in the year, too. Don't forget to consult your district's curriculum document and your school's official calendar. When are vacations? Professional development days? Standardized tests? School-wide special events?

It's always smart to tie these events into your curriculum somehow, if it seems natural to do so. For example, for Read Across America Day, the students at Stillmeadow School had a school-wide author celebration. Prior to the event, each student was given a blank book and was expected to have a completed project in time for the celebration. Teachers decided what they would be studying in February, with an eye toward that project. Some classes filled their blank books by writing memoirs. Some students wrote informational texts after studying many examples. Others wrote poetry anthologies.

## To Do

Brainstorm a comprehensive list of units of study, using any standards materials you are working with, as well as your stated goals in earlier chapters. What have you decided are the most important concepts to study? Is what you are planning part of accepted current best practices? In the next chapter, we'll take a closer look at each month and begin to translate this big-picture overview into usable plans for each unit.

# Yearly Overview Map WRITING

### UNIT OF STUDY TOPIC

**August**

**September**

**October**

**November**

**December**

**January**

**February**

**March**

**April**

**May**

**June**

There were specific reasons for some of the choices the teachers made. Their district curriculum calls for studying a variety of genres and for "producing and responding to literature," so they decided to cover those topics throughout the year. Several years ago, I worked with a group of teachers at Roberts Avenue School on a poetry unit of study. Specifically, we studied teaching poetry in the late fall while looking at the Writing Workshop in general. The teachers in this study group liked the way the unit worked for them and decided to include poetry in their plan for the following year as well.

Some teachers like to start their year with poetry because the lessons students learn carry over into the rest of the workshop (for example, close observation to detail, writing with voice, beginning with a feeling, and an awareness of craft and revision). Also, we've found that writers who may not be successful at other forms of writing seem to shine during a poetry study. Other teaches prefer to introduce poetry later in the year, during National Poetry Month in the spring. I know one school that has a school-wide poetry celebration in February. It makes sense for those classes to study poetry in January.

There is no wrong or right way to plan. When having conversations about best practices, we can decide if what we are doing is helping us be intentional in meeting the needs of our readers and writers.

As the sample plans show, no two plans will look the same. However, there may be some overlap. Now we'll take a look at plans for a reading curriculum.

### Yearly Overview Map WRITING
#### UNIT OF STUDY TOPIC

**September** Launching Storytelling
Building Community
Introducing Writer's Notebooks

**October** Personal Narrative
Writing "Small"

**November** Author's Craft

**December** Open Genres

**January** Revision/Editing

**February** CMT Prep

**March** Poetry

**April** Feature Articles

**May** Fiction

**June** Reflection and Plans for Summer Writing Projects

A third-grade writing plan may look something like this.

### *Identifying and Scheduling Units for the Reading Curriculum*

Think about the big ideas you may explore as a whole group in Reading Workshop. Again, you may want to refer back to the earlier chapters of this book and any additional research you may have done. Consider the following:

- sense of self as a reader/identity ("I'm the kind of reader who...")
- what it means to be a community of readers
- choosing just-right books and reading material
- using strategies to figure out words/using all sources of information
- strategies for understanding texts
- monitoring for understanding/detecting errors
- making connections (text-to-text, text-to-self, text-to-world)
- revisiting text to support ideas
- questioning authors and texts
- visualizing and inferring as we read
- determining what's important in what we read
- synthesizing and interpreting what we read

What are the topics/units of study in reading that you can imagine studying with your class?

_____

_____

_____

_____

_____

_____

_____

_____

_____

_____

_____

Now, decide what you will focus on each month. On the next page, fill in the Yearly Overview Map for your reading curriculum.

# Yearly Overview Map

| | CONNECTICUT, DISTRICT 6<br>Reading Focus | READING AND WRITING<br>Writing Focus |
|---|---|---|
| September | Sense of Self as Reader<br>Assessment Management<br>"Community of Readers"<br>What Are Good Readers?<br>Building Stamina<br>Monitoring<br>Book Choice | Sense of Self as Writer<br>Management<br>"Community of Writers"<br>What Are Good Writers?<br>Building Stamina<br>Basic Editing<br>Filling the Notebook |
| October | Monitoring for Understanding<br>Begin partnerships/grouping<br>for guided reading. | Gathering or Drafting<br>Notebook process as a group |
| November | Making Connections<br>3 ways of Connecting/Coding<br>Text (T-T,T-S, T-W)<br>Written Response | Memoir<br>Begin independent use<br>of notebook |
| December/<br>January | Questioning<br>Responding to my Questioning<br>Critical Reading | Writing for an Audience Revision<br>Letter Writing |
| January/<br>February | Visualizing/Inferring<br>Show, Not Tell | Writing with Clarity<br>Show, Not Tell<br>Elaboration and Detail<br>Genre: Poetry |
| February/<br>March | Determining Importance<br>Main Idea and Theme<br>Story Mapping<br>Character Mapping | Narrative Focus in Notebook<br>Author's Craft |
| April | Determining Importance | Nonfiction Writing |
| May | Synthesis | Notebook Use |
| June | Sense of Self as Reader<br>Plans for Summer Reading<br>Considering Identities and Goals<br>Reflecting on Growth | ... as Writer<br>Plans for Summer Writing<br>Reflecting on Growth |

Denise Bozutto, language arts coordinator for District 6 in Connecticut, put together this map for reading and writing that includes strategies from Harvey and Goudvis's *Strategies That Work: Teaching Comprehension to Enhance Understanding.* Think of your grade level and what you would keep or change in Bozutto's plan.

# Yearly Overview Map READING

## UNIT OF STUDY TOPIC

**August** _____

_____

**September** _____

_____

**October** _____

_____

**November** _____

_____

**December** _____

_____

**January** _____

_____

**February** _____

_____

**March** _____

_____

**April** _____

_____

**May** _____

_____

**June** _____

_____

# Points to Consider When Marking Your Calendar

While planning your year, keep in mind publication dates. You'll want to have at least 8 to 12 publication celebrations a year, which roughly translates to one per month. Usually when I tell teachers that, they groan. That's because we are accustomed to thinking about writing celebrations as full-blown tea parties, with parents and the public invited to see and hear typed-up, hardbound books created by our students. Those kinds of celebrations are nice, and I recommend them once or even twice a year, but certainly not ten times!

**To Do**

You may decide to create your yearly maps in a group. That doesn't mean that everyone will plan the same units at the same time. There are reasons to align your curriculum plans with colleagues and reasons not to. Discuss the pros and cons and come up with maps of your own.

How you celebrate at the end of a monthlong poetry unit will probably look very different from how you celebrate a two-week unit on revision. Where you may do something grand for poetry, a unit on revision may end with a student simply sharing with classmates how he "fixed up" his piece and made it stronger. In third grade, this may mean that a student added more details to his writing, in fourth grade, how he worked on his ending to make it more satisfying, and in fifth grade, how he added dialogue to his piece and worked on telling the internal story.

So, use ink to mark your calendar for publication dates and don't worry too much about how the students will publish. By setting up the dates before hand, you'll build structure around your workshops. I remember conducting a memoir genre study in my classroom. Even though we had been studying memoir for five weeks, I just didn't feel they were ready to publish. I dragged the study on for a few more weeks and, really, we didn't get much further. I began to run out of ideas and so did the students. We all got bored. When I started setting dates for publication though, we somehow managed to finish on time. I also learned to accept the fact that the work will never be perfect. We have to get what we can from each unit of study and move on.

Now that you have a yearly map in place, we can turn to Chapter 5 and focus on turning that map into monthly plans. Then, in Chapter 6, we'll take a close look at how those monthly plans can be translated into daily plans.

# A Closer Look

## Creating Monthly Plans

*Education is not about filling a bucket,
it is about lighting a fire.*

—John Taylor Gatto

**N**ow, here comes the fun part: converting those yearly overview maps into monthly plans. If you haven't done so already, create a tabbed divider page for each binder's month and/or unit sections, and then sort the materials you've collected so far. Use your divider pages to indicate what should go in each pile. Here's how one teacher labeled her tabbed sections:

Overview

Sept./Launching WW

Oct./Memoir

Nov./Poetry

Dec. through June . . .

Supplies/Wish List

Spelling/Word Work

Blackline Masters

Bibliographies

Assessment/Conferring

Sorting the resources you've gathered and reorganizing them into sections gives you easy access to materials when you create your weekly plans.

Many teachers find it helpful to take everything they've collected out of their binders and sort it on a large table. The floor works well, too! This alone could take up one of your scheduled study group meeting times. The Yearly Overview Maps, which you created in Chapter 4, should be the first pages in your binder, for easy reference. Some teachers use binders with clear plastic cover sleeves in which they place the Yearly Overview Maps (pages 95 and 99). This enables them to see the whole year at a glance.

You'll also be filling in a Unit Overview form for each section/month like the ones shown on page 103. Blank templates for writing and reading appear on pages 104 and 105. Photocopy enough templates for each unit you're planning and insert them in the appropriate sections of your binder.

Working collaboratively can make planning the year more focused and productive— and manageable.

## Writing Unit Overview

**Topic/Unit of Study:** *Launching Writing Workshop "Writerly Life"*     **Publication Date:** *4/27*

**Type of Publication/Celebration:** *various genres/share with small groups/bulletin board*

**Focus Lessons:**
*Storytelling (everyone has a story)*
*Writers write from their lives*
*Purpose of writing*
*Introduce notebooks, pocket folders, hanging files*
*"Rules" of writing workshop: routines materials use*

**Read Alouds:**
*Storytelling (everyone has a story)*
*Writers write from their lives*
*Purpose of writing*
*Introduce notebooks, pocket folders, hanging files*
*"Rules" of writing workshop: routines, materials use*

**Materials:**
*Samples of my own writing*
*Samples of students' writing*
*Notebooks*

**Home/School Connection: (homework)**
*Stories from home*
*Favorite books and authors*

**Assessment:**
*Spelling-writing sample for baseline, interest survey*

**Reflection:**

---

Samples of completed Unit Overview forms for reading and writing.

## Reading Unit Overview

**Strategy focus:** *Making Connections*     **Date:**

**Read Aloud (sample texts):**
*Koala Lou-Fox (reminders)*
*The Pain and the Great One-Blume (T-S)*
*Oliver Button is a Sissy-DePaola (T-T)*
*William's Doll-Zolotow (T-T)*
*The Keeping Quilt-Polacco (T-W)*
*Sarah Morton's Day/Samual Eaton's Day*
  *Tapenum's Day-Waters*

**Student Work:**
**During Read Aloud:**

*"say something" using sticky-notes in public tries, use journal or response sheet in public tries*

**During Independent Reading:**
*use sticky-notes to code connections and record a few words, use double-entry journals and quote, picture journal response pages (top is sticky-note or sketch from text, bottom is explanation of the connection, or story map)*

**Materials:**
*Journals or appropriate paper: double entry, quote or picture, top/bottom response pages, story map*

**Focus Lessons:**
*Think Alouds*
*Using background knowledge when reading (reminders)*
*Linking text to own life (text-to-self)*
*Connecting ideas across the text (text-to-text)*
*Linking text to science, social studies, understandings (text-to-world)*
*Identifying story elements*
*Identifying text structures in narrative and expository text*
*Explaining how the connection helped understanding*
*Identifying a word or words that support understanding*

**Shared/Guided Reading: (method)**
**Shared:** *story mapping*
        *Making social studies/science connections*
**Guided:**
*Locating connections and explaining understandings*

**Home/School Connection: (homework)**
*Rereading of days pages and completing a sticky-note or response entry*

**Assessment:**
*Running records, obervational notes, sticky-notes and response entries*

# Writing Unit Overview

**Topic/Unit of Study:**

**Type of Publication/Celebration:**

**Publication Date:**

**Focus Lessons:**

**Materials:**

**Read Alouds:**

**Home/School Connection: (homework)**

**Assessment:**

**Reflection:**

# Reading Unit Overview

Date:

Strategy focus:

Focus Lessons:

Read Aloud (sample texts):

Student Work:
During Read Aloud:

During Independent Reading:

Shared/Guided Reading: (method)
Shared:

Guided:

Home/School Connection: (homework)

Materials:

Assessment:

# Monthly Planning for Writing

To create plans that help us to be intentional, we need to consider all aspects of a good writing workshop. That way, we ensure that our focus lessons, materials, the type of publishing we do, and so forth support our units of study. Teachers who plan this way find that they are no longer jumping from one focus lesson to the next because they have a clear sense of where they're going for the duration of the study. Notice how the issues below closely parallel sections in the Unit Overview form.

## Issues to Consider When Planning Writing Workshop

- Topic/Unit of Study: what the students will be studying
- Mini-Lesson Focus: modeling/demonstrating—may focus on qualities of good writing or structures and rituals
- Publication type and date, based on the work students are doing daily leading to publication
- Materials
- Use of Literature/Read Aloud
- Home-School Connection (homework)
- Assessment Tools/Conferring/Ways to Differentiate Instruction
- Reflection

## To Do

Make several copies of the Writing Unit of Study: Initial Planning Sheet (or use the reading form if you are planning your reading units of study). Decide how you or your group will complete the work.

### Filling Out Unit Overview Forms

How do you decide what to include on the overview forms? It may be helpful to do some thinking on paper first—use the Initial Planning Sheets for writing and reading units of study (pages 107 and 110). Since you will be filling one out for each unit, you'll need to make a dozen or so photocopies. The information you fill in will be transferred to the Unit Overview form for each unit. If you are working in a study group, you may find it helpful to complete one or two of these sheets together. Then, do the rest of them on your own or assign them to individual colleagues. At your next meeting, you can share, revise, and edit.

# Writing Unit of Study
## INITIAL PLANNING SHEET

Date: _____          Unit of Study: _____

**Things to think about when planning the unit of study:**

What are the *most important* ideas I want the students to learn about this topic?

_____

_____

_____

How does this fit in with my district's expectations? What expectations will my students be meeting through this unit?

_____

_____

_____

What Read Alouds would be best for this unit?

_____

_____

_____

What focus lessons are a must?

_____

_____

_____

How long will the unit take?

_____

What type of publishing celebration best fits this type of unit? Have I scheduled a celebration well in advance and let the students and parents know the date? If so, date of celebration: _____

_____

_____

## Writing Unit of Study
### INITIAL PLANNING SHEET   *3rd Grade*

Date: _April_                              Unit of Study: _Poetry_

**Things to think about when planning the unit of study:**
What are the *most important* ideas I want the students to learn about this topic?
_doesn't have to rhyme_          _imagery/feeling/mood_
_close observation to detail_     _line breaks/white space/form_
_rhythm/voice/repetition_

How does this fit in with my district's expectations?  What expectations will my
students be meeting through this unit?
_third-grade curriculum—poetry   sense of self as writer_
_writing with description          revision/editing skills_

What Read Alouds would be best for this unit?
_"April Rain Song" by Langston Hughes_
_"Things" by Eloise Greenfield_
_Previous students' work_
_Poetry that kids collect and bring in from library, mostly non-rhyming_
_For the Good of the Earth and Sun by Georgia Heard_
_See attached lists_

What focus lessons are a must?
_beginning with a feeling_
_writing about something important     using line breaks and white space_
_close observation, writing with detail_
_describing something in a unique way, "beautiful language"_
_using line breaks and white space_

How long will the unit take?
_six weeks_

What type of publishing celebration best fits this type of unit?  Have I scheduled
a celebration well in advance and let the students and parents know the date?
If so, date of celebration: _first poems are typed_
_class anthology_
_poetry celebration paper_

---

## Writing Unit Overview

**Topic/Unit of Study:**     *Poetry*                              **Publication Date:**     *4/27*

**Type of Publication/Celebration:**     *poetry recital*

**Focus Lessons:**
| | |
|---|---|
| Gathering and Immersion | Line breaks/white space/form |
| Close Observation/Detail | Awareness of audience |
| Poetry doesn't have to rhyme | Reading aloud/performing |
| Rhythm/voice/repetition | Interpretation |
| Imagery/feeling/mood | Questioning |

**Materials:**
Transparencies of children's poetry
Georgia Heard's books
A Note Slipped Under the Door by McPhillips and Flynn
Artifacts from Nature
Samples of notebook entries reworked as poems

**Read Alouds:**
All kinds of poetry (mostly un-rhyming)
    see list in curriculum binder
"April Rain Song" by Langston Hughes
"Things" by Eloise Greenfield
Previous students' work

**Home/School Connection: (homework)**
Bring artifacts from home
Practice reading/reciting poetry
Bring poetry from home

**Assessment:**
Collect samples of students' work at beginning of unit and at end.
Look for evidence of voice, repetition, beautiful language.

**Reflection:**

---

To coincide with Poetry Month, a third-grade teacher may plan an April poetry unit of study as shown. The Initial Planning Sheet details the specifics of the plan, while the Unit Overview form shows the unit framework in a more general outline.

After you have completed a form for each of your units, place them in your binder in the appropriate sections. Now that you have focused your intentions for study, you may want to reorganize or eliminate materials that are currently in your binder. Start to collect examples of students' work to use at a later date. For example, if a student writes something that sounds like poetry during a revision unit, you can copy it and place it in your binder's poetry section for use later in a focus lesson. Or if you attend a workshop and get a great list of books for teaching memoir, put it in your binder's memoir section. You can also keep blackline masters of record-keeping forms that you have collected or developed. If you find great ideas for focus lessons in professional books or on Web sites, you can add them to the appropriate sections, too.

---

### Teacher Tip

Carla Monteiro, who teaches at the Tracey School in Norwalk, Connecticut, says this about collecting students' writing to use in focus lessons: "I can't describe how helpful it is to have samples of kids' work in my binder, right where I need them. I make copies and overheads of certain pieces that I know I will need, based on my yearly map. I can use the best samples year after year. It makes planning my daily focus lessons so much easier. I now confer differently, too, always looking for samples of students' work to use for lessons and knowing where to put them when I find them."

---

## Monthly Planning for Reading

We know that the best reading workshops provide opportunities for whole-group, small-group, and individual instruction delivered through the workshop components:

Read Aloud          Shared Reading

Independent Reading          Guided Reading

In Reading Workshop, what topics do you imagine studying as a whole class? Refer back to the Yearly Overview Map you created in Chapter 4. Then, as you did for Writing Workshop, fill out the Initial Planning Sheet on page 110 for each unit you intend to carry out. From there, transfer the information to the Unit Overview form for reading, on page 105.

# Reading Unit of Study
## INITIAL PLANNING SHEET

Date: _____          Unit of Study: _____

**Things to think about when planning the unit of study:**

What are the *most important* ideas I want the students to learn about this topic?

_____

_____

_____

_____

How does this fit in with my district's expectations? What expectations will my students be meeting through this unit?

_____

_____

_____

_____

What Read Alouds would be best for this unit?

_____

_____

_____

_____

_____

What focus lessons are a must?

_____

_____

_____

_____

How long will the unit take? _____

How will we wrap up this unit? What type of reflection will take place?

_____

_____

_____

_____

Unit end date: _____

## Reading Unit Overview

**Strategy focus:** *Monitoring for Understanding*        **Date:**

**Read Aloud (sample texts):**
*What You Know first–MacLachlan*
*When I Was Young in the Mountains–Rylant*
*How To Get Famous in Brooklyn–Hest*
*The Meet the Author Series–Richard C. Owen*
   *Publishers*
*Thank You, Mr. Falker–Polacco*
*The Bear Who Heard Crying–Kinsey–Warnick*

**Student Work:**
**During Read Aloud:**
*unfamiliar word/think*
*detect errors that do not make sense*
*detect confusing language/concepts*
*"say something"*

**During Independent Reading:**
*partner monitoring*
*coding the texts for confusions/unfamiliar words*
*strategy checklists*
*oral sampling or punctuation usage*
*coding the text for discussion spots*

**Materials:**
*Sticky-notes*    *A variety of books for*
*Running Record forms*   *book talk and choice*
*Note-taking forms*    *Self-evaluation forms*

**Focus Lessons:**
*Using all sources of information*
*Detecting errors*
*Problem-solving unknown words*
*Vocabulary/using content*
*Stopping when confused/rereading*
*Phrasing/fluency*
*Using punctuation to support understanding*
*Adjusting pace for purpose and difficulty*
*Inferring author's subtleties in text*
*Revisiting text to support ideas and understanding*
*book choice*

**Shared/Guided Reading: (method)**
**Shared:** *close procedure using a picture book*
*demonstrating, chunking*
*guided book choice (choice witin a selected text)*

**Guided:**
*word solving   fluency   rereading*

**Home/School Connection: (homework)**
*Rereading pages at home*
*Self-evaluation of strategy use*

**Assessment:** *Running records, observational notes, sticky-notes and response entries*

---

Here are two examples of Unit Overview forms for third-grade reading workshops, created by teachers in Connecticut's District 6.

## Reading Unit Overview

**Strategy focus:** *Making Connections*        **Date:**

**Read Aloud (sample texts):**
*Miss Rumphius–Coooney (T–S)*
*Giving Thanks–London (T–T)*
*The Gift of You, The Gift of Me (T–T)*
*The Quiltmaker's Gift–Brumbeau (T–T)*
*The Raft–LaMarche (T–T)*
*Roxaboxen–McLerran (T–W)*

**Student Work:**
**During Read Aloud:**

*"say something" using sticky-notes in public tries,*
*use journal or response sheet in public tries*

**During Independent Reading:**
*use sticky-notes to code connections and record a*
*few words, use double-entry journals and quotes,*
*picture journal response pages (top is sticky-note*
*or sketch from text, bottom is explanation of the*
*connection, or story map)*

**Materials:**
*Journals or appropriate paper: double entry, quote*
*or picture, top/bottom response pages, story map*

**Focus Lessons:**
*Think Alouds*
*Using background knowledge when reading (reminders)*
*Linking text to own life (text-to-self)*
*Connecting ideas across the text (text-to-text)*
*Linking text to science, social studies, understandings*
   *(text-to-world)*
*Identifying story elements*
*Identifying text structures in narrative and*
   *expository text*
*Explaining how the connection helped understanding*
*Identifying a word or words that support understanding*

**Shared/Guided Reading: (method)**
**Shared:** *story mapping*
        *Making social studies/science connections*
**Guided:**
*Locating connections and explaining understandings*

**Home/School Connection: (homework)**
*Rereading of days pages and completing a sticky-note*
*or response entry*

**Assessment:**
*Running records, obervational notes, sticky-notes and response entries*

---

Now that you have your monthly plans in place, it's time to start thinking about daily lesson plans. In Chapter 6, we'll consider how to use the monthly plans to create meaningful, organized daily lessons.

# What Do I Do Tomorrow?

## Translating Yearly and Monthly Plans into Daily Lessons

*By spending time focusing on our ultimate goals for the students, we've taken the guesswork out of creating daily mini-lessons. We're able to create focus lessons that make sense for the students and feel like they are part of a design, a bigger picture. No more deciding what to do tomorrow on a whim. In the past, the best workshop teachers knew how to do this instinctively, now we can all create cohesive, meaningful workshops.*

—Lynn Holcomb,
language arts coordinator,
Dobbs Ferry, New York

You've mapped out a year of units for reading and writing workshops. You've reflected on the most important aspects of each unit to come up with a monthly focus and plan. So I hope you are beginning to feel a sense of control over your workshop time. Isn't it comforting to know what you will be focusing on and when?

The next step is translating those yearly and monthly plans into daily focus lessons. We'll start by mapping out the weeks, and then get a sense of how each day's focus may go within units. Of course, you won't be able to plan 180 day's worth of lessons. That is not the nature of workshop teaching. But I will share some tips for planning by the week and suggestions for keeping daily lesson plans.

# Mapping Out the Weeks

The Weekly Planning Sheet on page 114 has proved helpful to many teachers. It is reminiscent of the Yearly Overview Map, but rather than breaking down the year by months, this sheet breaks down the month by weeks.

For each unit of study, certain focus lessons are a must. In fact, you specified many of these lessons in the Unit Overview forms that you filled out in Chapter 5. Look over your lists of focus lessons, unit by unit, and note the ones that make sense at the beginning. Which feel like they belong in the middle of the unit and which would be better at the end? Be sure to leave room for unplanned lessons—ones that need to be taught in response to the work the students are doing. And don't feel compelled to fill in every block. After all, some units will be six weeks long and some as few as two.

As you map out your weekly lesson plans, keep in mind all of the ways to get the information across to students, regardless of your topic. You can

- model your own reading and writing.
- tell them your point.
- share examples of students' work.
- share examples of published pieces.

Another way to get information across is by asking students to try what you are teaching. For example, to prepare for a focus lesson on writing strong leads, you can ask the students to try out a few options in their notebooks during a focus lesson. At the end of the short lesson, they may find that they have something to add to the draft on which they were working. The point is, it's important to "multiply" your lessons by revisiting a topic often and in a variety of ways. This is the kind of work we should be doing throughout the school year as we plan.

Sharing examples of published nonfiction is a key part of supporting students as they read and write in this genre.

# Weekly Planning Sheet

| | Monday | Tuesday | Wednesday | Thursday | Friday |
|---|---|---|---|---|---|
| Week 1 | | | | | |
| Week 2 | | | | | |
| Week 3 | | | | | |

# Weekly Planning Sheet

| | Monday | Tuesday | Wednesday | Thursday | Friday |
|---|---|---|---|---|---|
| **Week 4** | | | | | |
| **Week 5** | | | | | |
| **Week 6** | | | | | |

Remember, no matter what grade you teach, your first unit of study should have something to do with creating a community of readers and writers or helping students have a sense of themselves as readers and writers.

As the year goes on, as each unit comes to an end, you'll begin to look toward the next month's focus. Your units may overlap a bit at this stage—and that's okay. Toward the end of a unit on picture books, for example, the students may be spending their time putting finishing touches on their published pieces, while you are trying to get to everyone for an editing conference. During this time, it would make sense for your focus lessons to be related to publishing. At the same time, you can begin immersing the students in the next study—poetry for example. You can start collecting and reading poetry as a jump start.

In the process, you can fine-tune your poetry unit. Specifically, you can think about what would make sense at the beginning, middle, and end of the unit. You'll also be able to add lessons based on unanticipated needs. Do students still need work with using elaborative details? You may not have known this two months ago. That's why it's unwise to plan daily focus lessons too far in advance.

# Creating Daily Lesson Plans

It seems that every teacher of reading and writing for grades 3–5 has a different way of keeping daily lesson plans. When I was teaching, I tried several different lesson-plan books and systems before I came up with one that worked for me. I ended up creating my own blank schedule on the computer and printing one out for each day, on a monthly basis. Then, when I did my actual planning, I just filled in the blank spaces. Here's what the morning part of that schedule looked like:

| Time | Monday |
|------|--------|
| 8:45–9:00 A.M. | Independent Reading<br>Meet With: _____ |
| 9:10–9:40 A.M. | Meeting<br>Focus Lesson: _____<br><br>_____<br>_____<br>_____ |
| 9:45–10:45 A.M. | Reading Workshop (Unit of Study: _____ )<br>Independent Reading Focus: _____<br>Notes: _____<br><br>_____<br><br>Guided Reading Group: _____<br>Book Title/Level: _____<br>Instructional Focus: _____<br>Guided Reading Group: _____<br>Book Title/Level: _____<br>Instructional Focus: _____ |
| 10:45–11:30 A.M. | Writing Workshop (Unit of Study: _____ )<br>Focus Lesson: _____<br><br>_____<br>_____<br>_____ |
| 11:30–12:00 P.M. | Art |
| 12:00–12:35 P.M. | Lunch |

The weekly planning sheet on pages 118 and 119, reflect a fourth-grade literacy rich schedule. You might create a simple template like this and complete several, adding them to your curriculum binders before you begin each new unit.

| Time | Monday | Tuesday | Wednesday |
|------|--------|---------|-----------|
| **8:30–9:00 A.M.** | Independent Reading | Independent Reading | Independent Reading |
| **9:00–9:30 A.M.** | Morning Meeting (focus reading or writing unit of study: strategies/ independent work focus) | Morning Meeting (focus reading or writing unit of study: strategies/ independent work focus) | Morning Meeting (focus reading or writing unit of study: strategies/ independent work focus) |
| **9:30–11:00 A.M.** | Reading Workshop _____ _____ _____ _____ _____ _____ | Reading Workshop _____ _____ _____ _____ _____ _____ | Reading Workshop _____ _____ _____ _____ _____ _____ |
| **11:00–11:55 A.M.** | Writing Workshop Focus Lesson _____ _____ _____ | Writing Workshop Focus Lesson _____ _____ _____ | Writing Workshop Focus Lesson _____ _____ _____ |
| **11:55–12:25 P.M.** | Lunch | Lunch | Lunch |
| **12:25–12:55 P.M.** | Recess | Recess | Recess |
| **12:55–1:10 P.M.** | Read Aloud | Read Aloud | Read Aloud |
| **1:10–1:50 P.M.** | Media | Art | Gym |
| **1:50–2:45 P.M.** | Math obj. _____ _____ _____ _____ | Math obj. _____ _____ _____ _____ | Math obj. _____ _____ _____ _____ |
| **2:45–3:15 P.M.** | Social Studies or Science | Social Studies or Science | Social Studies or Science |

| Thursday | Friday | Notes |
|---|---|---|
| Independent Reading | Independent Reading | |
| Morning Meeting (focus reading or writing unit of study: strategies/ independent work focus) | Morning Meeting (focus reading or writing unit of study: strategies/ independent work focus) | |
| Reading Workshop <br> _____ <br> _____ <br> _____ <br> _____ <br> _____ <br> _____ | Reading Workshop <br> _____ <br> _____ <br> _____ <br> _____ <br> _____ <br> _____ | |
| Writing Workshop Focus Lesson <br> _____ <br> _____ <br> _____ | Writing Workshop Focus Lesson <br> _____ <br> _____ <br> _____ | |
| Lunch | Lunch | |
| Recess | Recess | |
| Read Aloud | Read Aloud | |
| Computers | Music | |
| Math <br> obj. _____ <br> _____ <br> _____ <br> _____ | Math <br> obj. _____ <br> _____ <br> _____ <br> _____ | |
| Social Studies or Science | Social Studies or Science | |

Deciding what to teach on a daily basis becomes so much easier when your monthly plan is in place. Try some of the ideas in this chapter and modify them as you see fit. Then share your plans with colleagues. There are many resources containing sample focus lessons. Refer to the list on page 61 for some helpful titles.

**Focus Lesson:** Making Connections—reminders
(written response to text)

**Read Aloud:** *The Relatives Came* by Cynthia Rylant
On large chart paper, teacher models using a double-entry journal, using yesterday's sticky-notes. Teacher thinks aloud the process.

**Student Work:**

**During Read Aloud**—Students "say something" to their Read Aloud partner that could be written for last few sticky-notes. Teacher records responses.

**During Independent Read**—Students continue coding their text with R and a few words. During last ten minutes of independent reading, students record in double-entry journals and share with a partner.

**During share**—Two to three students share model entries. Teacher reviews why it is important to make text-to-self connections when reading.

**Homework:** Reread pages you have read today and complete another double-entry journal entry.

A third-grade teacher's daily lesson plan for beginning a unit of study on making connections in reading.

Independent reading and writing times are gradually increased over the course of the year. At the beginning of the year, teachers spend time assessing individual readers and writers, and students may actually be reading independently for only about 15 minutes. Forty-five minutes is the goal towards late in the fall. If students are matched up with just-right texts, (books they can and want to read) then they will be able to sustain their reading for 45 minutes or longer! That time is used early in the year on Read Alouds.

# Chapter 7

# Reflections

*I'm still learning.*

—Michelangelo,
at the end of his life

**D**uring one of our last meetings of the school year, Kathy, Kay, and Michele (from Roberts Avenue School) and I reflected on the process of planning for the year. They had just finished their second year of teaching using units of study and curriculum binders. All three teachers agreed that they had never seen students grow so much in a single year. Kay attributed it to the fact that they got started right away with assessments. They didn't wait until the end of September. Planning and using the curriculum binder also helped them get their workshops up and running right away. For the first time, they started Writing Workshop and Independent Reading on the first day of school. By the end of September, they were amazed at how smoothly everything was running.

Having a yearly plan—and planning intentionally—helped them make sense of workshop teaching. A big relief for them was feeling like they didn't have to follow the teacher's manuals, page by page. These teachers felt empowered to make the right decisions for the students in their rooms. According to Kathy, "I no longer feel the pressure of wondering what I am going to do next." The children are central to her daily lesson planning because she has the framework of the units of study to keep her organized. Her focus has shifted.

At the end of each unit of study, they spent some time reflecting and making notes on their monthly planning sheets. What went really well during the unit? What will we do differently next time? They'll find that they will refer back to these notes while planning in the future.

At the end-of-the-year meeting, the teachers did decide to change a few things in their yearly plan. For example, they moved the poetry unit to a different month. And it was easy—they just opened the three-ring binder, took out the relevant material, and shifted it. They also planned some summer reading of professional books. All in all, they became used to the idea of thinking of themselves as researchers of teaching.

> *I never thought about these things when I considered planning before—my schedule, the room arrangement, materials….I feel so in control now, like my teaching makes sense.*
> —Kathy Hamilton,
> Roberts Avenue School

Planning for successful reading and writing is not something that you ever really finish. It is a work in progress, in need of constant refinement, as it should be. As you gain more knowledge by reading research-based materials, attending staff development programs, and learning with your students, you will add new information to your binders and curriculum plans. If this book has done nothing more than encourage you to view yourself as a researcher of teaching, then I've met my goal.

# Professional References Cited

Allington, R. (2005). *What really matters for struggling readers: Designing research-based programs* (2nd ed.). Upper Saddle River, NJ: Allyn & Bacon.

Atwell, N., & Newkirk, T. (Eds.). (1987). *Understanding writing: Ways of observing, learning, teaching.* Portsmouth, NH: Heinemann.

Calkins, L. (2001). *The art of teaching reading.* New York: Longman.

Fairfax Pubic Schools. (1995). *Primary purposes.* Fairfax, VA.

Fletcher, R., & Portalupi, J. (2001). *Writing workshop: The essential guide.* Portsmouth, NH: Heinemann.

Fountas, I., & Pinnell, G. (2001). *Guiding readers and writers, grades 3-6: Teaching comprehension, genre, and content literacy.* Portsmouth, NH: Heinemann.

_____. (1999). *Matching readers with books.* Portsmouth, NH: Heinemann.

Gentry, J. R. (2002). *The literacy map: Guiding children to where they need to be (Grades 4–6).* New York: Mondo.

Goodman, K. (1996). *On reading.* Portsmouth, NH: Heinemann.

Harvey, S., & Goudvis, A. (2000). *Strategies that work: Teaching comprehension to enhance understanding.* York, ME: Stenhouse Publishers.

Keene, E., & Zimmermann, S. (1997). *Mosaic of thought: teaching comprehension in a reader's workshop.* Portsmouth, NH: Heinemann.

National Academy of Education. (1985). *Becoming a nation of readers: The report of the Commission on Reading.* Pittsburgh, PA.

National Center for Education and the Economy (NCEE). (1999). *Reading and writing grade by grade: Primary literacy standards.* Washington, DC.

Ray, K.W. (1999). *Wondrous words: Writers and writing in the elementary classroom.* Urbana, IL: National Council of Teachers of English.

_____. (2001). *The writing workshop: Working through the hard parts (and they're all hard parts).* Urbana, IL: National Council of Teachers of English.

Routman, R. (2002). *Reading essentials: The specifics you need to teach reading well.* Portsmouth, NH: Heinemann.

_____. (2004). *Writing essentials: Raising expectations and results while simplifying teaching.* Portsmouth, NH: Heinemann.

Schulman, M. B., & Payne, C. (2000). *Guided reading: Making it work.* New York: Scholastic.

Smith, F. (1985). *Reading without nonsense.* New York: Teachers College Press.

Snowball, D. (1999). *Spelling k–8: Planning and teaching.* York, ME: Stenhouse.

Taberski, S. (2000). *On solid ground: Strategies for teaching reading.* Portsmouth, NH: Heinemann.

Trelease J. (2006). *The read-aloud handbook.* (6th ed.). New York: Penguin.

Weaver, C., Gillmeister-Krause, L., & Vento-Zogby, G. (1996). *Creating support for effective literacy education: Workshop materials and handouts.* Portsmouth, NH: Heinemann.

Wilhelm, J. (2001). *Improving comprehension with think-aloud strategies: Modeling what good readers do.* New York: Scholastic.

Wrubel, R. (2002). *Great grouping strategies.* New York: Scholastic.

# Children's Books Cited

Anthony, J. (1997). *The dandelion seed*. Nevada City, CA: Dawn Publications.

Brinkloe, J. (1986). *Fireflies*. New York: Aladdin.

Bunting, E. (1989). *The Wednesday surprise*. New York: Clarion Books.

Cooney, B. (1982). *Miss Rumphius*. New York: Viking Press.

Garland, S. (1993). *The lotus seed*. San Diego, CA: Harcourt Brace Jovanovich.

In Their Own Words (series). New York: Scholastic.

LaMarche, J. (2000). *The raft*. New York: HarperCollins.

Lisle, J. (1989). *The afternoon of the elves*. New York: Orchard Books.

_____. (1994). *The gold dust letters: The investigators of the unknown, Book 1*. New York: Orchard Books.

_____. (1999). *The lost flower children*. New York: Philomel Books.

Locker, T. (1995). *Sky tree*. New York: HarperCollins.

MacLaclan, P. (1994). *All the places to love*. New York: HarperCollins.

Nesbitt, E. (2004). *Five children and it*. New York: Harper Festival.

Osborne, M. The Magic Tree House (series). New York: Random House.

Rylant, C. (1996). *Whales*. New York: Blue Sky Press.

Sachar, L. (1994). *Marvin Redpost: Alone in his teacher's house*. New York: Random House.

# Index

# Notes